FTCE Physical Education K-12
Teacher Certification Exam

By: Sharon Wynne, M.S.
Southern Connecticut State University

Edited: Deborah Stuber, MS

XAMonline, INC.
Boston

Copyright © 2008 XAMonline, Inc.
All rights reserved. No part of the material protected by this copyright notice may be reproduced or utilized in any form or by any means, electronic or mechanical, including photocopying, recording or by any information storage and retrievable system, without written permission from the copyright holder.

To obtain permission(s) to use the material from this work for any purpose including workshops or seminars, please submit a written request to:

XAMonline, Inc.
21 Orient Ave.
Melrose, MA 02176
Toll Free 1-800-509-4128
Email: info@XAMonline.com
Web www.xamonline.com
Fax: 1-781-662-9268

Library of Congress Cataloging-in-Publication Data

Wynne, Sharon A.
  Physical Education K-12: Teacher Certification / Sharon A. Wynne. -2nd ed.
  ISBN 978-1-58197-616-8
    1. Physical Education K-12.   2. Study Guides.   3. FTCE
    4. Teachers' Certification & Licensure.   5. Careers

Disclaimer:

The opinions expressed in this publication are the sole works of XAMonline and were created independently from the National Education Association, Educational Testing Service, or any State Department of Education, National Evaluation Systems or other testing affiliates.

Between the time of publication and printing, state specific standards as well as testing formats and website information may change that is not included in part or in whole within this product. Sample test questions are developed by XAMonline and reflect similar content as on real tests; however, they are not former tests. XAMonline assembles content that aligns with state standards but makes no claims nor guarantees teacher candidates a passing score. Numerical scores are determined by testing companies such as NES or ETS and then are compared with individual state standards. A passing score varies from state to state.

Printed in the United States of America œ-1

FTCE: Physical Education K-12
ISBN: 978-1-58197-616-8

TEACHER CERTIFICATION STUDY GUIDE

Florida Teacher Certification Exams

Florida offers two types of Educator Certificates: the Temporary Certificate and the Professional Certificate.

Requirements:

Specialization Requirements for Certification in Physical Education (K-12):
1. A bachelor's or higher degree with a teacher education major in physical education, or
2. A bachelor's or higher degree with thirty semester hours in physical education to include the areas specified below:
    A. Twelve semester hours in instructional design and content of physical education,
    B. Motor development,
    C. Kinesiology,
    D. Administration of physical education,
    E. Applied exercise physiology,
    F. Adaptive or physical education for exceptional students,
    G. Care and prevention of human injures, and
    H. Theory and practice in coaching.

Temporary Certificate
(The Temporary Certificate is valid for three school years and is nonrenewable. It allows time to complete the requirements for a Professional Certificate while teaching full-time.)
1. Complete all application process requirements,
2. Hold at least a bachelor's degree, and
3. Demonstrate mastery of subject area knowledge or meet subject specialization with a 2.5 GPA for a requested subject.

The Professional Certificate
(The Professional Certificate is valid for five school years and is renewable. It is Florida's highest educator certificate.)
1. Complete all application process requirements,
2. Hold at least a bachelor's degree,
3. Demonstrate mastery of subject area knowledge for a requested subject,
4. Demonstrate mastery of general knowledge, and
5. Demonstrate mastery of professional preparation and education competency.

TEACHER CERTIFICATION STUDY GUIDE

About the FTCE in Physical Education:
The FTCE is composed of three tests: Professional Education, General Knowledge, and Subject Area Exams.

1. Professional Education – This multiple choice test assesses general knowledge of pedagogy and professional practices. It consists of 120 items and is usually given in the afternoon beginning at 1:00 pm. Testing time is 2 ½ hours.

2. Subject Area Exam – Subject exams measure content area knowledge, usually in multiple choice formats. It is generally given in the morning (8:30 am-noon).Testing time is 2 ½ hours. Candidates applying for a Professional Certificate must pass an exam to teach in a given field.

3. General Knowledge Test – This basic skills achievement test contains four subtests: Mathematics (multiple-choice), Reading (multiple-choice; passage-based), English Language Skills (multiple-choice), and an essay. This test requires applicants to arrive at 8:00 am and depart at 1:15 pm. Subtests may be registered for and taken separately. No other test may be taken on the same day.

The FTCE dealing with Special Education is also available on the computer. Registration is done online. Applicants may not retake any test prior to 31 days after their first testing date.

TEACHER CERTIFICATION STUDY GUIDE

Table of Contents

COMPETENCY 1.0   KNOWLEDGE OF THE HISTORY AND PHILOSOPHY OF PHYSICAL EDUCATION AS A PROFESSION 1

SKILL 1.1   Identify historical events and trends that have influenced the profession 1

SKILL 1.2   Relate goals and values for physical education to the philosophies of education that they reflect 3

COMPETENCY 2.0   KNOWLEDGE OF CURRICULAR THEORY AND DEVELOPMENT 5

SKILL 2.1   Identify the characteristics of various curriculum models 5

SKILL 2.2   Identify various factors to consider in curriculum planning, such as students' time, environment, equipment, facilities, space, and community resources 5

SKILL 2.3   Identify ways that national and state documents, standards, benchmarks, trends, and philosophies can be used to design and develop curricula 7

SKILL 2.4   Identify principles of long- and short-term planning to maximize learner participation and success 8

SKILL 2.5   Identify common concepts and content within physical education and other curriculum areas that promote interdisciplinary learning ... 8

COMPETENCY 3.0   KNOWLEDGE OF INSTRUCTIONAL STRATEGIES 10

SKILL 3.1   Identify strategies and adaptations that meet the needs of a diverse student population 10

SKILL 3.2   Identify various organizational strategies that promote maximum participation 12

SKILL 3.3   Identify teaching styles, communication delivery systems, and materials that facilitate learning 13

SKILL 3.4   Identify and apply motivational theories and techniques that enhance student learning 15

SKILL 3.5   Apply developmentally appropriate instructional strategies, techniques, and teaching methods that promote student learning 16

SKILL 3.6	Identify a variety of self-assessment and problem-solving strategies inherent in reflective teaching	17
SKILL 3.7	Identify the role of feedback in facilitating learning	18

COMPETENCY 4.0 KNOWLEDGE OF HUMAN GROWTH, MOTOR DEVELOPMENT, AND MOTOR LEARNING RELATED TO PHYSICAL ACTIVITY ... 20

SKILL 4.1	Determine the relationship between human growth and development and appropriate physical activity	20
SKILL 4.2	Apply learning and human development theories to construct a positive learning environment that supports psychomotor, cognitive, and affective development	20
SKILL 4.3	Apply motor development and motor learning principles to the acquisition of motor skills	23

COMPETENCY 5.0 KNOWLEDGE OF SKILL AND MOVEMENT PRINCIPLES IN PHYSICAL ACTIVITY ... 24

SKILL 5.1	Identify and apply the concepts of spatial awareness, body awareness, relationships, and effort qualities as they relate to movement forms	24
SKILL 5.2	Identify the fundamental movement patterns, including locomotor, nonlocomotor, and manipulative skills, as applied to movement forms	25
SKILL 5.3	Identify sequentially progressive activities that promote the acquisition of psychomotor, cognitive, and affective skills	26
SKILL 5.4	Identify appropriate cues, prompts, and strategies for teaching motor skills	28
SKILL 5.5	Apply mechanical principles of motion to movement forms	29
SKILL 5.6	Identify strategies to develop correct skill performance	39
SKILL 5.7	Analyze the mechanics of a skill or sequence of movements and identify ways in which the performer can improve the performance	40
SKILL 5.8	Identify how components of skill-related fitness affect performance	42

TEACHER CERTIFICATION STUDY GUIDE

COMPETENCY 6.0 KNOWLEDGE OF HEALTH AND WELLNESS AND ITS RELATIONSHIP TO PHYSICAL ACTIVITY 44

SKILL 6.1 Analyze health-related components of physical fitness 44

SKILL 6.2 Interpret data from physical fitness assessments for diagnosis and prescription 45

SKILL 6.3 Identify personal fitness programs that incorporate health-related components 47

SKILL 6.4 Identify components of nutrition 48

SKILL 6.5 Demonstrate knowledge of the relationship of nutrition and exercise in meeting the health needs of all students 51

SKILL 6.6 Identify health risks that can be reduced by physical activity 51

SKILL 6.7 Apply basic training principles and guidelines to improve physical fitness 53

SKILL 6.8 Identify exercises that benefit the major muscle groups of the body 58

SKILL 6.9 Identify how the structure and function of the human body adapt to physical activity 71

SKILL 6.10 Identify the physiological, psychological, and sociological benefits of physical activity 72

SKILL 6.11 Identify the contributions that physical education makes to lifelong physical activity and wellness 73

SKILL 6.12 Identify community resources that promote lifelong physical activity and wellness 74

COMPETENCY 7.0 KNOWLEDGE OF PRINCIPLES OF SOCIAL AND EMOTIONAL DEVELOPMENT THROUGH PHYSICAL ACTIVITY 75

SKILL 7.1 Identify the role physical activity can play in developing an understanding of diversity and cultural differences among people 75

SKILL 7.2 Identify the role physical activity plays in developing affective skills 76

COMPETENCY 8.0 KNOWLEDGE OF DEVELOPMENTALLY APPROPRIATE ASSESSMENT 77

SKILL 8.1 Identify assessment techniques, including authentic and traditional methods, for appropriate use within the cognitive domain 77

SKILL 8.2 Identify assessment techniques, including authentic and traditional methods, for appropriate use within the affective domain 77

SKILL 8.3 Identify assessment techniques, including authentic and traditional methods, for appropriate use within the psychomotor domain 79

SKILL 8.4 Select appropriate assessment strategies for curriculum design, lesson planning, student prescription, and program evaluation 80

SKILL 8.5 Interpret results of assessment for curriculum design, lesson planning, student prescription, and program evaluation 82

SKILL 8.6 Select methods of assessment appropriate for an inclusive environment 83

COMPETENCY 9.0 KNOWLEDGE OF SUPERVISION, MANAGEMENT, AND LAWS AND LEGISLATION THAT APPLY TO THE LEARNING ENVIRONMENT 84

SKILL 9.1 Identify procedures for selecting and maintaining appropriate equipment and facilities to enhance student learning 84

SKILL 9.2 Identify organizational strategies that enhance classroom management 86

SKILL 9.3 Identify supervisory and behavioral management techniques that enhance student learning 86

SKILL 9.4 Determine appropriate action for the care and prevention of injuries in physical education 87

SKILL 9.5 Identify major federal and state legislation that impacts physical education 89

SKILL 9.6 Identify areas of legal liability applicable to physical education 90

SKILL 9.7 Identify guidelines and actions that promote safety 92

TEACHER CERTIFICATION STUDY GUIDE

COMPETENCY 10.0 KNOWLEDGE OF APPROPRIATE RULES, STRATEGIES, AND TERMINOLOGY 90

SKILL 10.1 Apply appropriate rules and strategies of play to game and sport situations 90

SKILL 10.2 Identify terminology for various physical education activities............97

COMPETENCY 11.0 KNOWLEDGE OF PROFESSIONAL DEVELOPMENT AND ADVOCACY STRATEGIES 119

SKILL 11.1 Identify physical education professional organizations and activities that promote professional development............119

SKILL 11.2 Identify current professional literature, research, and other sources of information that enhance professional growth 119

SKILL 11.3 Identify ways to advocate the goals, objectives, and values of a comprehensive physical education program 120

COMPETENCY 12.0 KNOWLEDGE OF TECHNOLOGY 122

SKILL 12.1 Identify current technological resources for accessing information on physical activity and health...............122

SKILL 12.2 Identify appropriate uses of technology in the instructional process 123

SAMPLE TEST 127

ANSWER KEY...............154

RIGOR TABLE 155

RATIONALES WITH SAMPLE QUESTIONS 156

TEACHER CERTIFICATION STUDY GUIDE

Great Study and Testing Tips!

What you study in order to prepare for the subject assessments is the focus of this study guide, but equally important is *how* you study.

You can increase your chances of mastering the information in this study guide by taking some simple but effective steps.

Study Tips:

1. Eat foods that aid the learning process. Foods such as milk, nuts, seeds, rice, and oats help your study efforts by releasing natural memory enhancers called CCKs (*cholecystokinin*) composed of *tryptophan*, *choline*, and *phenylalanine*. All of these chemicals enhance the transmission of signals by neurotransmitters associated with memory. Before studying, try a light, protein-rich meal of eggs, turkey, and fish. All of these foods release the memory enhancing chemicals. The better the connections between neurons, the more information you comprehend and can remember.

Before you take a test, stick to a light snack of relaxing and energy boosting foods. A glass of milk, a piece of fruit, or some peanuts release various memory-boosting chemicals which can help you to relax and focus on the subject at hand.

2. Learn to take great notes. A by-product of modern culture is that we've grown accustomed to obtaining information in small doses (e.g. TV news "sound bites", or newspaper article synopses).

Consequently, we have subconsciously trained ourselves to assimilate information in neat little packages. If notes are scrawled all over your paper the flow of the information will likely be fragmented. Strive for clarity. Your notes will much clearer if you use a structured format. One very effective method for taking notes is called the *"Cornell Method"* described below.

Take a sheet of loose-leaf lined notebook paper and draw a vertical line from the top to the bottom of the paper about 1-2" from the left-hand edge.

Draw a horizontal line across the paper about 1-2" up from the bottom. Repeat this process on the reverse side of the page.

Examine the format. Note that there is ample room for notes, a left-hand margin for recording items that require special emphasis, or supplementary data from the textbook. There is a large area at the bottom of the page for a brief summary, and a small rectangular space for anything else you might want to record.

3. Get the concept and then the details. Too often we focus on the details and fail to develop an understanding of the concept. However, if you simply memorize dates, places, or names, you may miss the whole point of the subject.

A key to understanding ideas is to put them into your own words. If you are working from a textbook, summarize each paragraph you read in your mind. If you are outlining text, don't simply copy the author's words.

Restate them in your own words. You remember your own thoughts and words much better than someone else's, and subconsciously tend to associate the important details with the core concepts.

4. Ask why? Use questions to pull apart written material paragraph by paragraph. Evaluate headings and don't forget the captions under illustrations.

Example: If the heading is "Stream Erosion", flip it around to read "Why do streams erode?" Then answer the questions.

Training your mind to think in a series of questions and answers, will not only help you learn more, but will also reduce test anxiety since you will be accustomed to answering questions.

5. Read for reinforcement and future retrieval. Even if you only have 10 minutes to study, grab your notes or a book to read. Your mind is similar to a computer; you have to input data in order to process it. *By reading, you are creating the neural connections for future retrieval.* The more times you read something, the more you reinforce learning the ideas.

Even if you don't fully understand something on the first read, *your mind stores much of the material for later recall.*

6. Relax to learn, so go into exile. Our bodies respond to a unique inner biological clock. Burning the midnight oil works for some, but not for everyone.

If possible, set aside a particular place to study that is free of distractions. Shut off the television, cell phone, pager and ask friends and family members to refrain from disturbing you during your study period.

If total silence bothers you, try playing some soft background music. Studies show that light classical music played at a low volume aids in concentration.

Lyric-free music that evokes pleasant emotions is highly recommended. Try listening to just about anything by Mozart. You may find that it relaxes you.

TEACHER CERTIFICATION STUDY GUIDE

7. Use arrows not highlighters. At best, it's difficult to read a page full of yellow, pink, blue, and green streaks.

Try staring at a neon sign for a while and you'll soon see my point. The mass of colors obscure the message.

A quick note, a dash of color, an underlined word or phrase, or an arrow pointing to a passage is much clearer than a conglomeration of highlighted words.

8. Budget your study time. Although you shouldn't ignore any of the material, *allocate your available study time in the same ratio that topics may appear on the test.*

TEACHER CERTIFICATION STUDY GUIDE

Testing Tips:

1. Get smart, play dumb. Don't read anything into the question. Don't make an assumption that the test writer is looking for something other than what is asked. Stick to the question as written and don't read extra things into it.

2. Read the question and each choice *twice* before answering. You may miss important details by not carefully reading and re-reading the question and the answers.

If you really don't have a clue as to the right answer to a given question, leave it blank the first time through. Go on to complete the other questions, as they may provide clues about to how to answer the skipped questions.

If later on, you go back to a skipped question and still can't answer it . . . ***guess.*** The only penalty for guessing is that you *might* get it wrong. One thing is certain; if you don't put anything down, you will definitely get it wrong!

3. Turn the question into a statement. Look at the way the questions are worded. The syntax of the question usually provides a clue about the answer. Does it seem more familiar as a statement rather than as a question? Does it sound strange?

By turning a question into a statement, you may be able to spot if an answer sounds right, or it may trigger memories of material you've read.

4. Look for hidden clues. It's actually very difficult to compose multiple-choice questions without giving away part of the answer in the choices presented.

In most multiple-choice questions you can often readily eliminate one or two of the potential answers. This leaves only two real possibilities, and automatically your odds of selecting the right answer go to fifty-fifty with very little work.

5. Trust your instincts. For every fact that you have read, you subconsciously retain something of that knowledge. On questions that you aren't really certain about, go with your basic instincts. **Your first impression about how to answer a question is usually correct.**

6. Mark your answers directly on the test booklet. Don't bother trying to fill in the optical scan sheet on the first pass through the test. *However, be careful not to mark your answers in error when you transcribe them to the scan sheet.*

7. Watch the clock! You have a set amount of time to answer the questions. Don't get bogged down trying to answer a single question at the expense of 10 questions you can answer more readily.

THIS PAGE BLANK

TEACHER CERTIFICATION STUDY GUIDE

COMPETENCY 1.0   KNOWLEDGE OF THE HISTORY AND PHILOSOPHY OF PHYSICAL EDUCATION AS A PROFESSION

SKILL 1.1   Identify historical events and trends that have influenced the profession.

Germany, Sweden and England greatly influenced the early development of Physical Education, particularly from the late 1700's to the mid 1800's. Turner Societies were introduced to the states by German immigrants. Turner Societies advocated a type of system of gymnastics training that employed or utilized heavy equipment (e.g., horizontal and parallel bars, side horse) in their striving for fitness. In contrast, the Swedish preferred attaining and maintaining fitness through the use of light equipment. Their system of exercise promoted health through systematic movements with light equipment (e.g., ropes, climbing and wands). The English brought to sports and games to America. The sports and games they introduced emphasized moral development through participation in physical activities.

The first school to require physical education in its curriculum was The Round Hill School, in 1823. It was a private school in Northhampton, Massachusetts. After this, and continuing throughout the 1800's, the inclusion of physical education into the curriculum was prevalent in schools across America . The "first American to design a program of exercise for American children" (Lumpkin, Angela. 1994. *Physical Education and Sport: A contemporary Introduction*, 3rd edition. St. Louis: Mosby. pg. 202.) was developed in 1824 by Catherine Beecher. Ms. Beecher was the founder of the Hartford Female Seminary. The physical education curriculum that Ms. Beecher designed consisted of what we would refer to today as calisthenics. She was extremely active in promoting the inclusion of physical education into the public school curriculum. It took until 1855, for this to happen, when Cincinnati, Ohio became the first city school system to offer physical education to students in public schools.

California was the first state to pass a law, in 1866, that actually required two periods a day of exercise in its public schools. During this time, specifically between 1855 and 1900, Ms. Beecher, along with her contemporaries, Edward Hitchcock, Dudley Allen Sargent and Dio Lewis were the early leaders in physical education. Debates abounded as to whether it was best to use the system they had established in America, or systems advocated by the Germans, Swedes or English as a way of providing a national physical education program for America. These debates were referred to as the *Battle of Systems*.

Throughout the 1890's and during this period of great debate, John Dewey challenged the traditional education system. Mr. Dewey and his colleagues are responsible for expanding the education system based on the "three R's", to include physical education in America. It was also during this time in history that many schools of higher education began to offer training for physical education teachers. Because of the strong emphasis on the sciences, including physiology and anatomy, many professors training the students held medical degrees.

In 1893, Thomas Wood stated that "the great thought of physical education is not the education of the physical nature, but the relation of physical training to complete education, and then the effort to make the physical contribute its full share to the life of the individual." (National Education Association. 1893. *NEA Proceedings* 32: 621. pg.621.)This was the beginning of a change in thinking about the importance of physical education with regard to the overall education of the American children. Many early twentieth century educational psychologists, including John Dewey, Edward Thorndike, and Stanley Hall, supported Wood's line of thinking and the important role of play in furthering children's ability to learn. As a result, in 1927, *The New Physical Education* was published by Wood and Rosalind Cassidy, also a strong advocate of education through the physical.

Charles McCloy agreed with Wood's and Cassidy's thinking and published work, however he believed that physical education did more than just contribute to the overall well-being and learning abilities of children. He held that physical education's primary objective was and is the development of skills as well as the maintenance of the body. His views expanded on Wood's and Cassidy's theories. The testing of motor skills was a significant aspect of McCloy's contribution to physical education. Additionally, his philosophy of testing motor skills paralleled the scientific movement in education during this time period.

In the early 1920's many states passed legislation that required physical education in the schools. This trend continued until the 1950's when, eventually, all states required physical education in their schools. The curriculum of physical education changed as the events in the country occurred. For example, during World War II, the emphasis in physical education shifted from games to physical conditioning. In 1953, the President's Council on Physical Fitness was established when it was noted through the Kraus-Weber study that American children were far less fit than children in European countries. The council was established to assist the falling fitness levels of America's children and youth.

SKILL 1.2 Relate goals and values for physical education to the philosophies of education that they reflect.

The various philosophies of education greatly influence the goals and values of physical education. Important educational philosophies related to physical education are Idealism, Realism, Pragmatism, Naturalism, Existentialism, Humanism, and Eclecticism.

Idealism – The **mind**, developed through the acquisition of knowledge, is of highest importance. Values exist independently of individuals. Fitness and strength activities contribute to the development of one's personality. Horace Mann, Wadsworth, Kant, Plato, and Descartes were Idealists.

Realism – The physical world is **real.** A realist believes in the laws of nature, the scientific method, and mind and body harmony. Religion and philosophy co-exist. Physical fitness results in greater productivity, physical drills are important to the learning process, athletic programs lead to desired social behavior, and play and recreation help life adjustment. Aristotle was a realist.

Pragmatism – **Experience** is the key to life. Dynamic experience shapes individuals' truth. Education is child-centered. Consequently, Physical Education takes the form of creating physical activities and sports for children to experience and thus discover.

Varied physical and sports activities present meaningful, socializing experiences. Problem-solving accomplishes learning. Both John Dewey and Charles Pierce were pragmatists.

Naturalism – This philosophy is materialistic. Things that actually exist are found only within the physical realm of nature. Nature is valuable. The individual is more important than society. Self-activities accomplish learning and activities are more than physical in nature. Naturalists promote play and discourage high levels of competition. Physical education takes a holistic approach.

Existentialism – The chief concern is **individualism.** Existentialists do not want the individual to conform to society. They promote freedom of choice and a variety of interests. Individuals need to have their own system of values. Playing develops creativity and the discovery of the "inner self." Sartre, Soren, and Kierkegaard were Existentialists.

Humanism and **Eclecticism** – These are the modern philosophies of physical education followed by most schools today. The Humanistic philosophy is based on the development of individual talents and total fulfillment that encourages involvement and participation in one's environment. Humanists encourage self-actualization and self-fulfillment. Curriculums based on the Humanistic approach are student-centered. The Eclectic approach combines beliefs from different philosophies. When different philosophies are blended skillfully, the Eclectic approach affords a sound philosophy for developing individuals.

TEACHER CERTIFICATION STUDY GUIDE

COMPETENCY 2.0   KNOWLEDGE OF CURRICULAR THEORY AND DEVELOPMENT

SKILL 2.1 Characteristics of various curriculum models.

With a history that spans centuries and has roots traceable to the ancient Greeks, physical education include techniques that help in promoting the physical fitness and well-being of a body.

The primary aim of physical education, otherwise known as physical training, is to equip students with the knowledge, skills, capabilities, values, and enthusiasm necessary to the maintenance of a healthy lifestyle into adulthood, regardless of physical ability. Activities are included to promote physical fitness, develop motor skills, instill knowledge and understanding of rules, concepts, and strategies, and teach students to work as part of a team or as individuals in a wide variety of play-based and competitive activities.

Physical education has come to occupy a very important role in most school programs. There are various curriculum models for physical education courses. Such curricula stress the meaning of human movement, physiology of exercise, sport sociology, aesthetic appreciation of movement, and the acquisition of skills. Modern curricula include all of these competencies.

The modern physical education curriculum provides students a basic experience in the following activities: aquatics, conditioning, gymnastics, individual/dual sports, team sports, and rhythm and dance. All states in the United States offer physical education to students in grades K through 12, and many states require the self-contained classroom teacher to implement a physical education program.

All curriculum models have the following characteristics: physical activity, by which students will become competent in a variety of, and proficient in a few, physical activities; human movement, in which students will understand and apply principles of human movement to the learning and development of motor skills; fitness; responsible behavior, wherein students will exhibit responsible personal and social behavior in physical activity settings; respect for differences; and benefits of physical activity, by which students will identify and understand how physical activity provides personal enjoyment, challenge, self-expression, and social interaction.

SKILL 2.2   Identify various factors to consider in curriculum planning, such as students' time, environment, equipment, facilities, space, and community resources.

CLASS MANAGEMENT TECHNIQUES TO ENHANCE LEARNING

The first few weeks of the school year is the most effective time to teach class management structures (e.g. behavioral rules, terms for compliance, consequences for violating rules, and classroom routines).

Instructors must manage essential class structures, procedures, and routines (e.g. roll call, excuses, tardiness, changing clothes, and showering) in order to use class time efficiently. Good class management ensures the safety of the group through consistent procedures and routines which provides a controlled atmosphere making instruction easier. Consistent class management procedures and routines promote self-discipline and self-motivation. They encourage a sense of responsibility towards others, help establish rapport between teacher and students, create group camaraderie, and ultimately serve to organize classes for the most effective instruction and learning.

Long-term planning for the semester and year, as well as daily, weekly, and seasonally, is necessary. Instructors must effectively plan activities so that they proceed with precision, minimize "standing-around time", and allow for maximum activity time for each student. Instructors should arrange activities in advance and prepare any necessary line markings.

To determine student progress and assess the effectiveness of teaching, instructors must apply appropriate measurement and evaluation techniques. Instructors also must wear suitable clothing, have thorough knowledge of the subject, and promote appropriate attitudes toward and understandings of fitness, skill learning, sportsmanship, and other physical education objectives.

USING EQUIPMENT, FACILITIES, SPACE, AND COMMUNITY RESOURCES

In addition to providing a safe, education-friendly environment that maximizes the productive use of class time, physical education instructors must effectively use equipment, facilities, space, and community resources.

Instructors must have a thorough understanding of athletic equipment to demonstrate its proper usage and ensure student safety during activities. Instructors should expose students to a variety of activities and corresponding equipment. Instructors must also consider the feasibility of certain activities as determined by the availability and cost of required equipment.

Instructors must consider available facilities and space when planning physical education curriculum. Facilities and space may limit the types of activities students can engage in. For example, sports like golf require large open spaces and specific equipment that schools may not have.

Physical education instructors should investigate and research community resources. Community organizations and athletic clubs will often provide schools with equipment, facilities, and volunteer instructors for free or at reduced fees.

SKILL 2.3　Identify ways that national and state documents, standards, benchmarks, trends, and philosophies can be used to design and develop curricula.

Physical education instructors can use national and state documents, standards, benchmarks, trends and philosophies to design and develop effective curricula.

First, governmental organizations (e.g. U.S. Department of Education, individual state departments of education) regularly release documents outlining standards for physical education. Common physical education standards require that students learn skills necessary to participate in a variety of physical activities, become physically fit, participate regularly in physical activity, understand the benefits and implications of physical fitness, and value physical activity as part of a healthy lifestyle. Instructors must mold their curricula to ensure that their students meet these standards.

In addition, governmental organizations often determine benchmarks that define physical development and fitness in school-age children. For example, standards may indicate what motor skills students should possess at certain ages and the specific performance criteria that define physical fitness. Instructors can use the benchmarks and tests to evaluate student development and fitness and plan curricula for student improvement.

Finally, national trends and philosophies greatly affect physical education curricula. National trends toward greater longevity, increased obesity, and sedentary lifestyles demand a renewed emphasis on fitness and activity to prevent and reduce obesity and lifestyle-related health problems. The philosophies of lifelong learning and fitness are an important aspect of physical education. Instructors should design curricula that encourage and motivate students to become active and to develop a lifelong interest in the physical health of their bodies.

TEACHER CERTIFICATION STUDY GUIDE

SKILL 2.4 **Identify principles of long- and short-term planning to maximize learner participation and success.**

Both long- and short-term planning are important aspects of effective curriculum design. Physical education instructors must make short-term plans (e.g. one day, one week) that maximize learner participation and success.

For example, instructors should plan an appropriate variety of activities that will appeal to the interests and abilities of the students and promote some level of success for each student. In addition, appropriate rotations of students, planned before each class, allows for maximum participation and limits downtime.

Long-term planning (e.g. one month, one unit, or one semester) allows instructors to build a comprehensive, sequential curriculum that promotes the development of student skills, fitness, and knowledge over time. For example, an elementary instructor may plan a sequence of units starting with basic running and jumping skills and ending with the introduction of organized sports activities.

SKILL 2.5 **Identify common concepts and content within physical education and other curriculum areas that promote interdisciplinary learning.**

Physical education is a key component of an interdisciplinary learning approach because it draws from many other curriculum areas. Instructors can relate concepts from the physical sciences, mathematics, natural sciences, social sciences, and kinesiology to physical education activities.

Physical science is a term for the branches of science that study non-living systems. However, the term "physical" creates an unintended, arbitrary distinction, since many branches of physical science also study biological phenomena. Topics in physical science such as the movement of an object through space and the effect of gravity on moving objects are of great relevance to physical education. Physical sciences allow us to determine the limits of physical activities.

Mathematics is the search for fundamental truths in pattern, quantity, and change. Examples of mathematical applications in sport include measuring speed, momentum, and heights of objects; measuring distances and weights; scorekeeping; and statistical computations.

Natural science is the study of living things. Content areas in the natural sciences of great importance to physical education include physiology, nutrition, anatomy, and biochemistry. For example, a key component of physical education is an understanding of proper nutrition and the affect of food on the body.

PHYSICAL EDUCATION K-12

The social sciences are a group of academic disciplines that study human behavior in the world. Social scientists engage in research and theorize about aggregate and individual behaviors. For example, a basic understanding of psychology is essential to the discussion of human patterns of nutrition and attitudes toward exercise and fitness. Sport psychology is a specialized social science that explores the mental aspects of athletic performance.

Finally, kinesiology encompasses human anatomy, physiology, neuroscience, biochemistry, biomechanics, exercise psychology, and sociology of sport. Kinesiologists also study the relationship between the quality of movement and overall human health. Kinesiology is an important part of physical therapy, occupational therapy, chiropractics, osteopathy, exercise physiology, kinesiotherapy, massage therapy, ergonomics, physical education, and athletic coaching. The goal of these applications may be therapeutic, preventive, or attaining high-performance. The application of kinesiology can also incorporate knowledge from other academic disciplines such as psychology, sociology, cultural studies, ecology, evolutionary biology, and anthropology. The study of kinesiology is often part of the physical education curriculum and illustrates the truly interdisciplinary nature of physical education.

COMPETENCY 3.0   KNOWLEDGE OF INSTRUCTIONAL STRATEGIES

SKILL 3.1   Identify strategies and adaptations that meet the needs of a diverse student population.

One of the most challenging aspects of being a teacher is the need to provide a curriculum that uses strategies and adaptations to meet the needs of a diverse student population. Schools have made huge strides in meeting these needs through the use of resource teachers trained to work specifically with students who have varying exceptionalities.

The law requires that teachers and schools provide the "least restrictive environment" for all students. The students to whom this law applies in particular have Individualized Educational Plans, or IEPs. These students have diverse needs. Identification of the "least restrictive environment" for them is done during annual meetings (or during the school year as needed) that include the resource teacher, all the classroom teachers, including the P.E. teacher and the parents. In the upper grades, such as high school, at the parent's discretion, the student may attend these meetings.

Specific strategies involve:

- Arranging peer-to-peer activities. For example, if a student is unable to shoot a basketball correctly, train a peer who can to assist the student.

- Grouping students by skill levels.

- Setting up station rotations where diverse exposure to activities is allowed.

- Bringing in the student's resource teacher to assist the student as needed.

ADAPTING SELECTED ACTIVITIES

Specific strategies involve:

Walking: adapt distance, distance over time, and number of steps in specified distance; provide handrails for support; change slope for incline walking; and change width of walking pathway.

Stair climbing: change pathway, pace, and number and height of steps.

Running: change distance over time, use an incline-changing slope (distance over time), and form a maze (distance over time).

Jumping: change distance and height of jump, change distance in a series and from a platform, change participants' arm positions.

Hopping: change distance for one and two hops (use preferred and non-preferred leg) and distance through obstacle course.

Galloping: change number of gallops over distance, change distance covered in number of gallops, widen the pathway.

Skipping: change number of errorless skips, change distance covered in number of skips, number of skips in distance, add music for skipping in rhythm.

Leaping: change distance and height of leaps.

Bouncing balls: change size of ball (larger), have participant use two hands, reduce number of dribbles, bounce ball higher, have participant remain stationary and perform bounces one at a time.

Catching: use larger balls and have participant catch balls thrown at chest level from a lower height of release, shorten catching distance, have participant stop and then catch ball (easier than moving and catching).

ADAPTING FOR STRENGTH, ENDURANCE, AND POWER PROBLEMS

Specific strategies involve:

1. Lowering basketball goals or nets; increasing size of targets.

2. Decreasing throwing distance between partners, serving distance, and distance between bases.

3. Reducing size or weight of projectiles or balls to be thrown.

4. Shortening length and/or reducing weight of bat or other striking apparatus.

5. Playing games in lying or sitting positions to lower center of gravity.

6. Selecting a "slow ball" (one that will not get away too fast), deflating ball in case it gets away, or attaching a string to the ball for recovery.

7. Reducing playing time and lowering number of points to win.

8. Using more frequent rest periods.

9. Rotating often or using frequent substitution when needed.

10. Using mobilization alternatives, such as using scooter boards one inning/period and feet for one inning/period.

ADAPTING FOR BALANCE AND AGILITY PROBLEMS

Specific strategies involve:

1. Using chairs, tables, or bars to help with stability.
2. Having participants learn to utilize eyes optimally for balance skills.
3. Teaching various ways to fall and incorporating dramatics into activities.
4. Using carpeted surfaces.
5. Lowering center of gravity.
6. Having participant extend arms or providing a lightweight pole.
7. Having participant keep as much of his/her body in contact with the surface.
8. Widening base of support (distance between feet).
9. Increasing width of walking parameters.

ADAPTING FOR COORDINATION AND ACCURACY

Specific strategies involve:

Throwing Activities: using beanbags, yarn or small foam balls, and/or smaller-sized balls.

Catching and Striking Activities: using larger, softer, and lighter balls; throwing balls to mid-line; shortening distance; and reducing speed of balls.

Striking/Kicking Activities: enlarging striking surfaces, choking up on bats, beginning with participant successfully striking stationary objects and then progressing to striking with movement, and increasing target size.

EXERCISE PHYSIOLOGY ADAPTATIONS

Decreasing the amount of weight, amount of reps/sets, pace, and/or distance of exercise; increasing the amount of intervals; and combining together any of the previous modifications.

SKILL 3.2 Identify various organizational strategies that promote maximum participation.

There are three options for maximizing participation: activity modification, multi-activity designs, and homogeneous or heterogeneous grouping.

Activity modification is the first option to achieve maximum participation by simply modifying the type of equipment used (i.e. substitute a yarn ball for a birdie for badminton) or the activity rules. However, keep the activity as close to the original as possible.

Multi-activity designs permit greater diversification of equipment and more efficient use of available facilities (keeps all students involved).

Homogeneous and heterogeneous grouping allows for individualized instruction, enhances students' self-concepts, equalizes competition, and promotes cooperation among classmates.

Plan activities that encourage maximum participation by utilizing all available facilities and equipment, involve students in planning class work/activities, and be flexible. Instructors can also use tangible rewards including praise to encourage maximum participation.

SKILL 3.3   Identify teaching styles, communication delivery systems, and materials that facilitate learning.

TEACHING STYLES

Common teaching styles that physical education instructors use to facilitate learning are: command style, practice style, reciprocal style, and inclusion style.

Command style requires that the teacher make all decisions and control all the activities. The command style is particularly useful in teaching students a skill in a short period of time. Because command style allows very little student-teacher and student-student interaction, instructors should limit its use to initial demonstrations and explanations.

Practice style allows students to make decisions and move at their own skill level during the implementation phase of skill development. Practice style is particularly useful when students have achieved basic skill competency because it allows self-paced practice and individualized feedback.

Reciprocal style involves the interaction of pairs of students. Reciprocal style provides needed social interaction and allows students to learn from each other through observation. The instructor is also free to interact with the students.

Inclusion style gives all students the chance to participate in the same task regardless of skill level. Students decide how to best go about practicing and developing their skills. They learn their strengths and weaknesses through trial and error. For example, when learning to throw objects at a target, students can choose the size and type of target and the distance between themselves and the target that best suits their ability level.

COMMUNICATION DELIVERY SYSTEMS

Three basic types of communication delivery systems relevant to physical education are written, verbal, and visual.

Written communication is particularly effective when communicating large amounts of information. In addition, instructors may choose to provide students with written instructions for classroom activities to eliminate the need for extended and repeated explanations.

Verbal communication is traditionally the foundation of teacher-student interaction. Verbal communication is an effective method when explaining skills and concepts. Physical education instructors should try to limit verbal instructions and explanations to allow for maximum physical activity during class time.

Visual communication is an important, and often underutilized, method of communication in physical education. Visual demonstrations are often the most effective way to introduce athletic skills and activities.

MATERIALS THAT FACILITATE LEARNING

Successful physical education teachers use many different materials to enhance the learning process. We discuss the effective and appropriate use of physical education materials– including sports equipment, safety equipment, and literature– elsewhere in this text.

SKILL 3.4 Identify and apply motivational theories and techniques that enhance student learning.

Motivation is essential to student learning in physical education and all academic disciplines. Physical education instructors should recognize and understand the important elements of student motivation. Important theories and concepts in student motivation include attribution theory, social learning theory, learned helplessness, and self-efficacy.

Attribution theory describes how people form causal explanations and how they answer questions that begin with "Why?" The theory deals with the information people use in making causal inferences and with how they utilize this information to answer causal questions. For instance, a student's aggressively competitive behavior may be a reflection of her personality, or it may be a response to situational pressures. Attribution theory describes the processes of explaining events and the behavioral and emotional consequences of those explanations. Attribution theory also claims that students' perceptions about their educational experience affects their motivation more than the experience itself.

Social learning theory focuses on the learning that occurs within a social context. It emphasizes that people learn from one another and includes such concepts as observational learning, imitation, and modeling. Social learning theory asserts that people can learn by observing the behavior of others and the outcomes of those behaviors. It further states that learning can occur without a permanent change in behavior. Physical education instructors should also note that cognition plays an important role in learning. Awareness and expectations of future rewards or punishments can have a major effect on the behaviors that people exhibit. Thus, socialization and reward/punishment can motivate students to learn.

Learned helplessness occurs in situations where continued failure may inhibit somebody from trying again and can also lead to many forms of depression. Thus, how physical education instructors respond to children's failures and successes is very important. If a student feels as though he cannot control his environment, this perceived lack of control will impair learning in certain situations. That is, learned helplessness often occurs in environments in which people experience events over which they have, or feel as though they have, no control over what happens to them.

Self-efficacy describes a person's belief about his/her capability to perform at designated levels in order to exert influence over events that affect their lives. Self-efficacy beliefs determine how people feel, think, motivate themselves, and behave. Such beliefs produce these diverse effects through cognitive, motivational, affective, and selection processes. A strong sense of efficacy enhances human accomplishment and personal well-being in many ways. People with high assurance of their capabilities view difficult tasks as challenges rather than threats. A student with high self-efficacy will be highly motivated to participate in sports and game-related activities. To build efficacy, the instructor must not only raise the student's belief in his/her capabilities, but also structure situations that breed success and limit repeated failure. Students with high self-efficacy measure success in terms of self-improvement rather than by triumphing over others.

SKILL 3.5   Apply developmentally appropriate instructional strategies, techniques, and teaching methods that promote student learning.

Physical education instructors should employ a variety of instructional strategies, techniques, and teaching methods to promote student learning. Instructors must tailor their methods to match the age and developmental level of their students.

STRATEGIES THAT PROMOTE COMPETENCE IN PHYSICAL ACTIVITIES

Instructors must employ a variety of techniques to promote competence in physical activities. Instructors should use verbal instruction, demonstration, practice, and assessment.

Applying techniques that allow students to measure their competence is a useful strategy for physical education teachers. Some techniques include: mapping, using a checklist of skills broken into steps to check off once students have mastered each level of an activity or skill, and external rewards such as stars or other symbols displayed next to students' names on a posted chart.

It is important that instructors tailor their techniques to fit the age and skill level of their students. For example, activities for a third grade class will be much simpler than activities for a high school class. In addition, older, more developed students are better able to handle competitive situations than younger students. Younger and less skilled students require a cooperative, stress-free environment to maximize learning.

STRATEGIES THAT PROMOTE POSITIVE ATTITUDES TOWARD FITNESS

One of the most important tasks for physical education instructors is to instill in their students an appreciation of and a positive attitude toward physical fitness. Creating a safe and cooperative learning environment is the best strategy for fostering positive attitudes. Allowing students to explore activities, plan fitness goals, improve personal fitness levels, and generally take responsibility for their own physical fitness promotes a positive attitude toward lifelong fitness. Additionally, students need to be taught and have an understanding of the many benefits being physically fit provides. Providing opportunities to participate in many different types of physical activities allows for students to, hopefully find a sport or activity that they enjoy, and can continue throughout their lives.

STRATEGIES THAT INVOLVE STUDENTS WITH VARYING INTERESTS AND ABILITIES

(See Skill 3.1)

A major challenge that physical education instructors face is planning a curriculum that appeals to students of different ability levels and different interests. Instructors should provide students with a range of activities that appeal to students with varying interests. Instructors must use a creative approach to inspire students that may not have a natural interest in sports and fitness. Finally, instructors must tailor their lessons to accommodate students of varying abilities and developmental stages. Not all students will be able to perform the same skills and tasks.

SKILL 3.6 Identify a variety of self-assessment and problem-solving strategies inherent in reflective teaching.

The **Reflective Approach** to teaching involves continuous self-monitoring by the teacher, of situations, behaviors, practices, effectiveness, and accomplishments. The instructor reflects upon and evaluates his or her own teaching and determines what changes are necessary.

EVALUATE PERSONAL FITNESS PROGRAMS AND RECOMMEND CHANGES WHERE NEEDED

Personal fitness program design requires careful self-assessment and problem-solving. After assessing an individual's fitness level, an instructor can prescribe a personal fitness program. Prescription of a fitness program begins with:

1. Identifying components of fitness that need to be changed (via assessment).

2. Establishing short-term goals.

3. Developing a plan to meet the established goals.

4. Keeping records to monitor progress.

5. Evaluating progress toward meeting goals and making changes based on success or failure.

For successful programs, formulating new goals changes the personal fitness program to accomplish those new goals.

For unsuccessful programs, changing the goals, particularly if the goals were unrealistic, is appropriate for the individual to make progress and succeed. In addition, analyzing positive and negative reinforcements may identify barriers preventing an individual's success in his/her personal fitness program. Incorporating periodic, positive rewards for advancing can provide positive reinforcement and encouragement.

SKILL 3.7 Identify the role of feedback in facilitating learning.

Feedback, or input from the tutor or educator, forms an extremely vital part of any learning process. Just as positive feedback works as a motivator enabling an athlete to improve and surge ahead with renewed interest, negative feedback also helps an athlete recognize and correct his or her mistakes.

When performers learn a skill, the skill goes into their short-term memory and receives positive feedback. The skill may eventually go into their long-term memory, creating more permanent memory. That is how positive feedback works to encourage the performer and helps in making the performer remember every aspect of the performance.

Negative feedback helps athletes, whether novice or experienced, become conscious of their mistakes. They can use this negative feedback to improve their shortcomings. Without feedback, an athlete is not likely to improve their technique and they will lose motivation.

There are different types of feedback and it is always important for the performer to receive the right type. Some examples of feedback include the following:

Intrinsic feedback – information received by the athlete as a direct result of producing a movement through the kinesthetic senses – e.g. feeling from muscles, joints, and balance.

Extrinsic feedback – information not inherent in the movement itself but which improves intrinsic feedback (this is also known as augmented feedback).

There are two main categories: knowledge of performance and information about the technique and performance.

The coach can provide extrinsic feedback verbally or visually via video. Extrinsic feedback enables the athlete to establish a kinesthetic reference for performing the correct movement.

Research also indicates that the stage when an athlete receives feedback is as important as the content of the feedback. Negative feedback might be boring for the beginner. However, if a performer is elite, then knowledge of results is very important. In addition, during the cognitive stage, positive feedback is essential to make sure that a skill is learned successfully. Thus, feedback plays an extremely important role in any learning process, as it facilitates learning to a great extent.

COMPETENCY 4.0 KNOWLEDGE OF HUMAN GROWTH, MOTOR DEVELOPMENT, AND MOTOR LEARNING RELATED TO PHYSICAL ACTIVITY

SKILL 4.1 Determine the relationship between human growth and development and appropriate physical activity.

Understanding the rate of the developmental growth process that occurs during adolescence will help educators understand growth and development norms and identify early- or late-maturing students. The age when the puberty growth spurt occurs and the speed with which adolescents experience puberty vary greatly within each gender and may affect participation in physical activity and sports. If the instructor pays attention to the varying body sizes and maturity stages, forming teams in co-educational classes can easily accommodate the needs of both genders' changing maturities. Starting in middle school and continuing into high school, it is perfectly acceptable for boys and girls to participate in non-contact physical activities together that rely on lower-body strength and agility (e.g. capture the flag, ultimate Frisbee, running). In more physical activities that require upper body strength, coaches should form teams based on individual skill levels to prevent injury. Matching teams evenly based on skill and maturity is important so that individual skill level deficiencies are not as apparent and the activity remains fun for all participants. Teachers need to monitor and adjust physical activities as needed to ensure a positive, competitive experience. Appropriate activities would include individual or partner badminton or tennis matches and team competitions in flag football.

At the elementary school levels, students go to P.E. and primarily participate in activities that involve running, throwing, kicking, catching and tossing. These are basic skill development activities for this age group in physical education.

SKILL 4.2 Apply learning and human development theories to construct a positive learning environment that supports psychomotor, cognitive, and affective development.

Effective physical education programs support psychomotor, cognitive, and affective development.

Physical education through the Psychomotor Domain contributes to movement skills through participation and observation of sports and other physical activities; contributes to utilizing leisure hours in mental and cultural pursuits; contributes skills necessary to preserving the natural environment.

Physical education in the Cognitive Domain contributes to academic achievement; is related to higher thought processes via motor activity; contributes to knowledge of exercise, health and disease; contributes to an understanding of the human body; contributes to an understanding of the role of physical activity and sport in the American cultures; and contributes to the critical consumption of goods and services.

Physical education in the Affective Domain contributes to self-actualization, self-esteem, and a healthy response to physical activity; contributes to an appreciation of beauty; contributes to directing one's life toward worthy goals; emphasizes humanism; affords individuals the chance to enjoy rich social experiences through play; assists cooperative play; teaches courtesy, fair play, and good sportsmanship; contributes to humanitarianism.

Teaching methods to facilitate psychomotor learning include:

1. **Task/Reciprocal** - The instructor integrates task learning into the learning setting by utilizing stations.

2. **Command/Direct** - Task instruction is teacher-centered. The teacher clearly explains the goals, explains and demonstrates the skills, allocates time for practice, and frequently monitors student progress.

3. **Contingency/Contract** – An instructional style in which the teacher rewards students for the completion of tasks.

Techniques that facilitate psychomotor learning include:

1. **Reflex movements** - Activities that create an automatic response to some stimuli such as: flexing, extending, stretching, and postural adjustment.

2. **Basic fundamental locomotor movements** - Activities that utilize instinctive patterns of movement established by combining reflex movements.

3. **Perceptual abilities** - Activities that involve interpreting auditory, visual, and tactile stimuli in order to coordinate adjustments.

4. **Physical abilities** - Activities to develop physical characteristics of fitness in order to provide students with the stamina needed for highly advanced, skilled movements.

5. **Skilled movements** - Activities that involve instinctive, effective performance of complex movement including vertical and horizontal components.

6. **Nondiscursive communication** - Activities necessitating expression as part of the movement.

Teaching methods that facilitate cognitive learning include:

1. **Problem Solving** - The instructor presents the initial task and students come to an acceptable solution in unique and divergent ways.

2. **Conceptual Theory** - The instructor's focus is on acquisition of knowledge.

3. **Guided Inquiry** – Stages of instructions strategically guide students through a sequence of experiences.

Initially, performing skills will be variable, inconsistent, error-prone, "off-time," and awkward. Students' focus will be on remembering what to do. Instructors should emphasize clear communication of the skill's biomechanics and correct errors in gross movement that effect significant parts of the skill. So students will not be overburdened with too much information, they should perform one or two elements at a time. Motivation results from supportive and encouraging comments. Peer-to-peer encouragement is also very useful and helpful.

Techniques to facilitate cognitive learning include:

1. **Transfer of learning** – Identifying similar movements from a previously learned skill present in a new skill.

2. **Planning for slightly longer instructions and demonstrations** as students memorize cues and skills.

3. **Using appropriate language** for the level of the students.

4. **Conceptual thinking** - giving more capable students more responsibility for their own learning.

Aids to facilitate cognitive learning include:

1. **Frequent assessments** of student performance.

2. **Movement activities** incorporating principles of biomechanics.

3. **Utilization of technology**: e.g. laser discs, computers and software.

4. **Utilization of video recordings** of student performance.

Teaching methods and techniques that facilitate affective development include:

1. **Fostering a positive learning environment** – Instructors should create a comfortable, positive learning environment by encouraging and praising effort and emphasizing respect for others.

2. **Grouping students appropriately** – Instructors should carefully group students to best achieve equality in ability, age, and personalities.

3. **Ensuring all students achieve some level of success** – Instructors should design activities that allow students of all ability levels to achieve success and gain confidence.

SKILL 4.3   Apply motor development and motor learning principles to the acquisition of motor skills.

Motor-development learning theories that pertain to a general skill, activity, or age level are important and necessary for effective lesson planning. Motor-skill learning is unique to each individual, but does follow a general sequential skill pattern, starting with general gross-motor movements and progressing to specific or fine motor skills. Teachers must begin instruction at a level where all children are successful and proceed through the activity until frustration for the majority hinders the activity. Students need to learn the fundamentals or basics of a skill, or subsequent learning of more advanced skills becomes extremely difficult. Students must spend enough time on learning beginning skills so they become second nature.

Teaching in small groups with enough equipment for everyone is essential. Practice sessions that are too long or too demanding can cause physical and/or mental burnout. Teaching skills over a longer period of time, but with slightly different approaches, helps keep students attentive and involved as they internalize the skill. The instructor can then begin to teach more difficult skills while continuing to review the basics. If the skill is challenging for most students, allow plenty of practice time so that they retain it before having to use it in a game situation.

Visualizing and breaking the skill down mentally is another way to enhance the learning of motor movements. Instructors can teach students to "picture" the steps involved, and visualizing themselves executing the skill. First teach the skill by demonstrating the necessary steps. Beginning with the first skill taught, introduce key language terms and have students visualize performing the skill. For example, when teaching how to dribble a basketball, begin by demonstrating the skill and the component steps. Show students how to push the ball down toward the ground, let it bounce back up, and push it down again. Next, have students practice dribbling while standing still. Then have them add movement and practice dribbling. Finally, demonstrate how to control dribbling while being guarded by another student.

COMPETENCY 5.0   KNOWLEDGE OF SKILL AND MOVEMENT PRINCIPLES IN PHYSICAL ACTIVITY

SKILL 5.1   Identify and apply the concepts of spatial awareness, body awareness, relationships, and effort qualities as they relate to movement forms.

APPLY THE CONCEPT OF SPATIAL AWARENESS TO PHYSICAL EDUCATION ACTIVITIES

Spatial awareness is the ability to make decisions about an object's positional changes in space (i.e. awareness of three-dimensional space position changes).

Developing spatial awareness requires two sequential phases: 1) identifying the location of objects in relation to one's own body in space, and 2) locating more than one object in relation to each object and independent of one's own body.

Plan activities using balls, boxes, or hoops of different sizes and have children move towards and away; under and over; in front of and behind; inside and outside, and beside the objects.

APPLY CONCEPT OF BODY AWARENESS TO PHYSICAL EDUCATION ACTIVITIES

Body awareness is the awareness and understanding a person has of his or her own body parts and their capability of movement.

Instructors can assess body awareness by playing and watching a game of "Simon Says" and asking the students to touch different body parts. You can also instruct students to make their bodies into various shapes, from straight to round, to twisted, and varying sizes, to fit into different-sized spaces.

In addition, you can instruct children to touch one part of their body to another and to use various body parts to stamp their feet, twist their neck, clap their hands, nod their heads, wiggle their noses, snap their fingers, open their mouths, shrug their shoulders, bend their knees, close their eyes, bend their elbows, or wiggle their toes.

APPLY THE CONCEPT OF EFFORT QUALITIES TO PHYSICAL EDUCATION.

Effort qualities are the qualities of movement that apply the mechanical principles of balance, time, and force.

Balance - activities for balance include having children move on their hands and feet, lean, move on lines, and balance and hold shapes while moving.

Time - activities using the concept of time can include having children move as fast as they can and as slow as they can in specified, timed movement patterns.

Force - activities using the concept of force can include having students use their bodies to produce enough force to move them through space. They can also paddle balls against walls and jump over objects of various heights.

SKILL 5.2   Identify the fundamental movement patterns, including locomotor, nonlocomotor, and manipulative skills, as applied to movement forms.

IDENTIFY AND DEFINE LOCOMOTOR SKILLS

Locomotor skills move an individual from one point to another.

1. **Walking** - with one foot contacting the surface at all times, walking shifts one's weight from one foot to the other while legs swing alternately in front of the body.

2. **Running** - an extension of walking that has a phase in which the body is propelled with no base of support (speed is faster, stride is longer, and arms add power).

3. **Jumping** – projectile movements that briefly suspend the body in midair.

4. **Vaulting** - coordinated movements that allow one to spring over an obstacle.

5. **Leaping** - similar to running, but with greater height, flight, and distance.

6. **Hopping** - using the same foot to take off from a surface and land.

7. **Galloping** - forward or backward advanced elongation of walking combined and coordinated with a leap.

8. **Sliding** - sideward stepping pattern that is uneven, long, or short.

9. **Body Rolling** - moving across a surface by rocking back and forth, by turning over and over, or by shaping the body into a revolving mass.

10. **Climbing** - ascending or descending using the hands and feet with the upper body exerting the most control.

IDENTIFY AND DEFINE NONLOCOMOTOR SKILLS

Nonlocomotor skills are stability skills in which the movement requires little or no movement of one's base of support and does not result in a change of position.

1. **Bending** - movement around a joint where two body parts meet.

2. **Dodging** - sharp change of direction from an original line of movement such aaway from a person or object.

3. **Stretching** - extending/hyper-extending joints to make body parts as straight or as long as possible.

4. **Twisting** - rotating body/body parts around an axis with a stationary base.

5. **Turning** - circular movement of the body through space while releasing the base of support.

6. **Swinging** - circular/pendular movement of body/body parts below an axis.

7. **Swaying** - same movement as swinging but the movement is above an axis.

8. **Pushing** - applying force against an object or person to move it away from one's body or to move one's body away from the object or person.

9. **Pulling** - using force to cause objects/people to move toward one's body.

IDENTIFY AND DEFINE MANIPULATIVE SKILLS

Manipulative skills use body parts to propel or receive an object, controlling objects primarily with the hands and feet. Two types of manipulative skills are receptive (catch + trap) and propulsive (throw, strike, kick).

1. **Bouncing/Dribbling** - projecting a ball downward.

2. **Catching** - stopping the momentum of an object (for control) using the hands.

3. **Kicking** - striking an object with the foot.

4. **Rolling** - applying force to an object that retains contact with a surface.

5. **Striking** - giving impetus to an object using the hands or an object.

6. **Throwing** - using one or both arms to project an object into midair away from the body.

7. **Trapping** - without the use of the hands, receiving and controlling a ball.

SKILL 5.3 **Identify sequentially progressive activities that promote the acquisition of psychomotor, cognitive, and affective skills.**

IDENTIFY TECHNIQUES TO ENHANCE SKILL AND STRATEGY PERFORMANCE

Playing complex games requires the combination of skills, the use of skills in more complex ways, and relating to others in both offensive and defensive settings. Sequentially progressive activities allow students to acquire the psychomotor, cognitive, and affective skills necessary for participation in complex games. There are four stages of complex skill development.

Stage One concerns **controlling an object**. For striking or throwing objects, students can consistently practice sending objects to a specified location, developing control of the force that accomplishes the objective. For catching or collecting, students can practice control by securing possession of an object from any direction, level, or speed. For carrying and propelling, students can practice maintaining control of an object by moving in different directions and at different paces. Developing control begins with the completion of easily attainable objectives and progresses gradually to more difficult objectives involving movement and different directions, levels, and force.

Stage Two also concerns controlling an object, however, combining skills increases difficulty. Instructors should stress rules to constrain the execution of skills. Drills such as passing and dribbling belong in stage two.

Stage Three focuses on **offense and defense**, utilizing correct skill performance. Students should now be able to control objects; therefore, the focus shifts to obtaining and maintaining possession, as well as offensive and defensive strategies in the midst of opponents. Net activities and keep-away games help develop this stage. In addition, instructors can add more offensive and defensive players, boundaries, scorekeeping, and conduct rules. Students develop by adjusting their responses with each element introduced to the activity.

Stage Four involves **complex activity.** Students execute the complete activity and modified activities that allow participation by all students. Continuous play is important; thus, the instructor may have to modify rules or a part of the activity to keep the flow of the game constant (e.g. eliminating free throws/kicks, substituting volleyball serve with a throw, initiating play out-of-bounds).

SKILL 5.4 **Identify appropriate cues, prompts, and strategies for teaching motor skills.**

Cues – The physical education teacher should have training in kinesiology so he or she will know what cues to pay attention to. **See Skill 5.7.** When determining and relating appropriate cues, the following criteria are important.

1) The majority of students should be successful.

2) The students must respect the teacher, fellow students, the sport, the equipment, and the facilities.

3) The students must follow directions.

Prompts - The physical education teacher should use prompts to deliver consistent training related to using facilities, equipment, instructional signals and principles. When determining prompts, the following criteria are important.

1) The facilities - From the first minute a kindergarten student enters the gym the teacher trains them to line up on a line, take a seat on a spot, jump in place, reach for the sky, or follow the yellow lines. This training promotes early-stage body awareness.

2) The equipment – Use the ball itself as a prompt to show where to make contact, how to grip the football, where on the rim of a basketball hoop to aim, or where to drop the basketball on the backboard.

3) The whistle is the most easily identified prompt to start and stop an activity.

4) Kinesiology principles – The teacher demonstrates technique first, and then the students practice. The teacher motivates, then moves to refine student movements with various observations on how to perform a skill better using better body mechanics.

Strategies – The physical education teacher should use strategies to provide appropriate instruction, individualize instruction, and maintain a safe and enjoyable learning environment.

1) Demonstrate good form – Visualize the skill, use it in slow motion, and use technology when available. Have the students mimic the motion, add additional details such as height, force, intensity, duration, etc., add another person to the activity, and add groups to larger groups.

2) Physical education provides the opportunity for group instruction, but instructors should individualize the instruction when dealing directly with a student. The pace of skill development varies widely.

3) Treat teaching as and art and a science.

4) Give children a chance to lead because it builds self-esteem.

5) Keep groups as small when possible so children have as much contact with the equipment as possible.

6) Use all the available equipment when appropriate and safe.

7) Spread out using the available facility space for safety and fun.

8) Plan practice sessions that last a reasonable length of time based on the age of the students.

9) Reinforce lessons sequentially.

SKILL 5.5 Apply mechanical principles of motion to movement forms.

APPLY THE CONCEPT OF EQUILIBRIUM TO MOVEMENT

When segments of the body move independently, body mass redistributes, changing the location of the center of gravity. Segments also move to change the body's base of support from one moment to the next to cope with imminent loss of balance. The entire center of gravity of the body shifts in the same direction of movement of the body's segments.

As long as the center of gravity remains over the base of support, the body will remain in a state of equilibrium. The more the center of gravity is situated over the base, the greater the stability. A wider base of support and/or a lower center of gravity enhances stability. To be effective, the base of support must widen in the direction of the force produced or opposed by the body. Shifting weight in the direction of the force in conjunction with widening the base of support further enhances stability.

Constant interaction of forces that move the body in the elected direction results in dynamic balance. The smooth transition of the center of gravity changing from one base of support to the next produces speed.

APPLY THE CONCEPT OF FORCE TO MOVEMENT.

Force is any influence that can change the state of motion of an object; we must consider the objective of movement.

Magnitude of Force – force must overcome the inertia of the object and any other resisting forces for movement to occur.

For linear movement, force applied close to the center of gravity requires a smaller magnitude of force to move the object than does force applied farther from the center of gravity.

For rotational movement, force applied farther from the center of gravity requires a smaller magnitude of force to rotate the object than does force applied closer to the center of gravity.

For objects with a fixed point, force applied anywhere other than through the point of fixation results in object rotation.

Energy – the capacity to do work. (The more energy a body has the greater the force with which it can move something [or change its shape] and/or the farther it can move it).

Movement (mechanical energy) has two types:

1. Potential energy (energy possessed by virtue of position, absolute location in space or change in shape).

   A. Gravitational potential energy - potential energy of an object that is in a position where gravity can act on it.

   B. Elastic (strain) potential energy - energy potential of an object to do work while recoiling after stretching, compressing, or twisting.

2. Kinetic energy (energy possessed by virtue of motion that increases with speed).

Force Absorption - maintaining equilibrium while receiving a moving object's kinetic energy without sustaining injury or without losing balance while rebounding. The force of impact is dependent on an object's weight and speed. The more abruptly kinetic energy is lost, the more likely injury or rebound occurs. Thus, **absorbing force requires gradually decelerating a moving mass by utilization of smaller forces over a longer period of time**. Stability is greater when the force is received closer to the center of gravity.

Striking resistive surfaces - the force of impact per unit area decreases when the moving object's area of surface making contact increases and the surface area that the object strikes increases.

Striking non-resistive surfaces - the force of impact decreases if the moving object's area of surface making contact decreases as it is more likely to penetrate a non-resistive surface.

The more time and distance that motion stops for a moving object to strike any surface, the more gradually the surface absorbs the force of impact, and the reaction forces acting upon the moving object decrease.

Equilibrium returns easily when the moving body (striking a resistive surface) aligns the center of gravity more vertically over the base of support.

Angular force against a body decreases when the distance between a contacting object and the body decreases and the contact occurs closer to the center of gravity. Also, widening the base of support in the direction of the moving object increases a person's stability.

APPLY THE CONCEPT OF LEVERAGE TO MOVEMENT.

First-class lever - the axis is between the points of application of the force and the resistance.

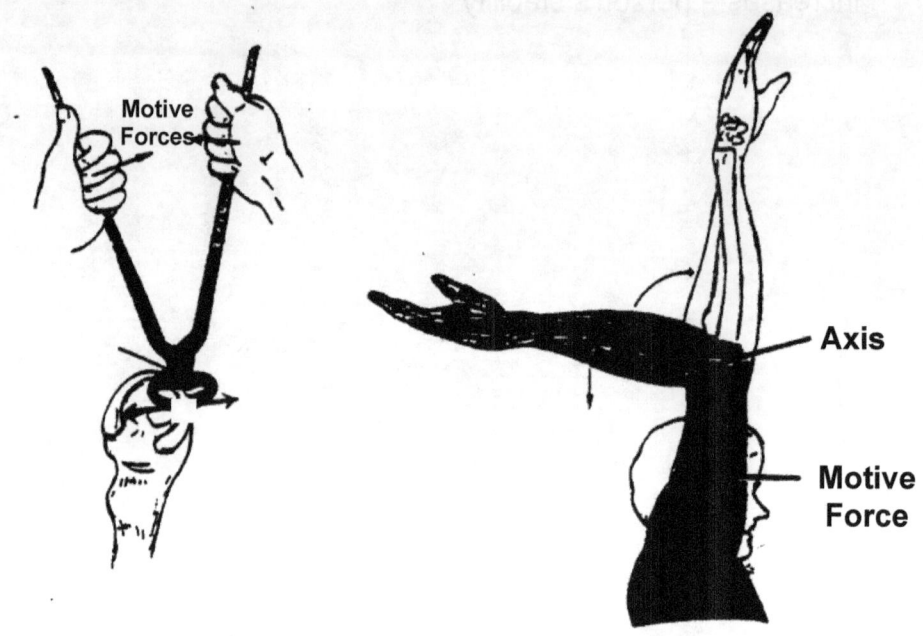

Second-class lever - the force arm is longer than the resistance arm (operator applies resistance between the axis and the point of application of force).

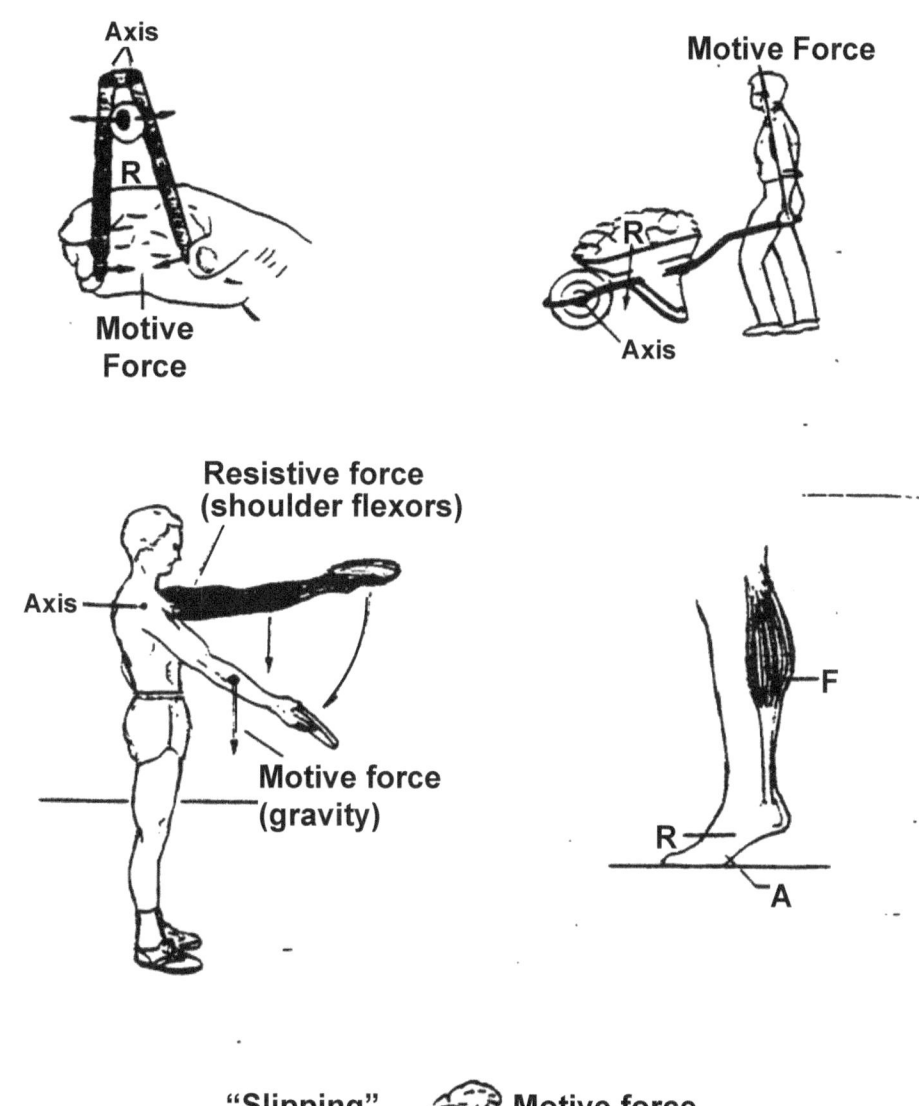

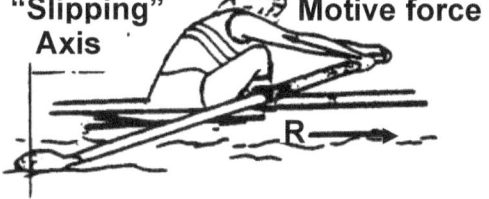

Second-class lever systems

Third-class lever - the force works at a point between the axis and the resistance (resistance arm is always longer than the force arm).

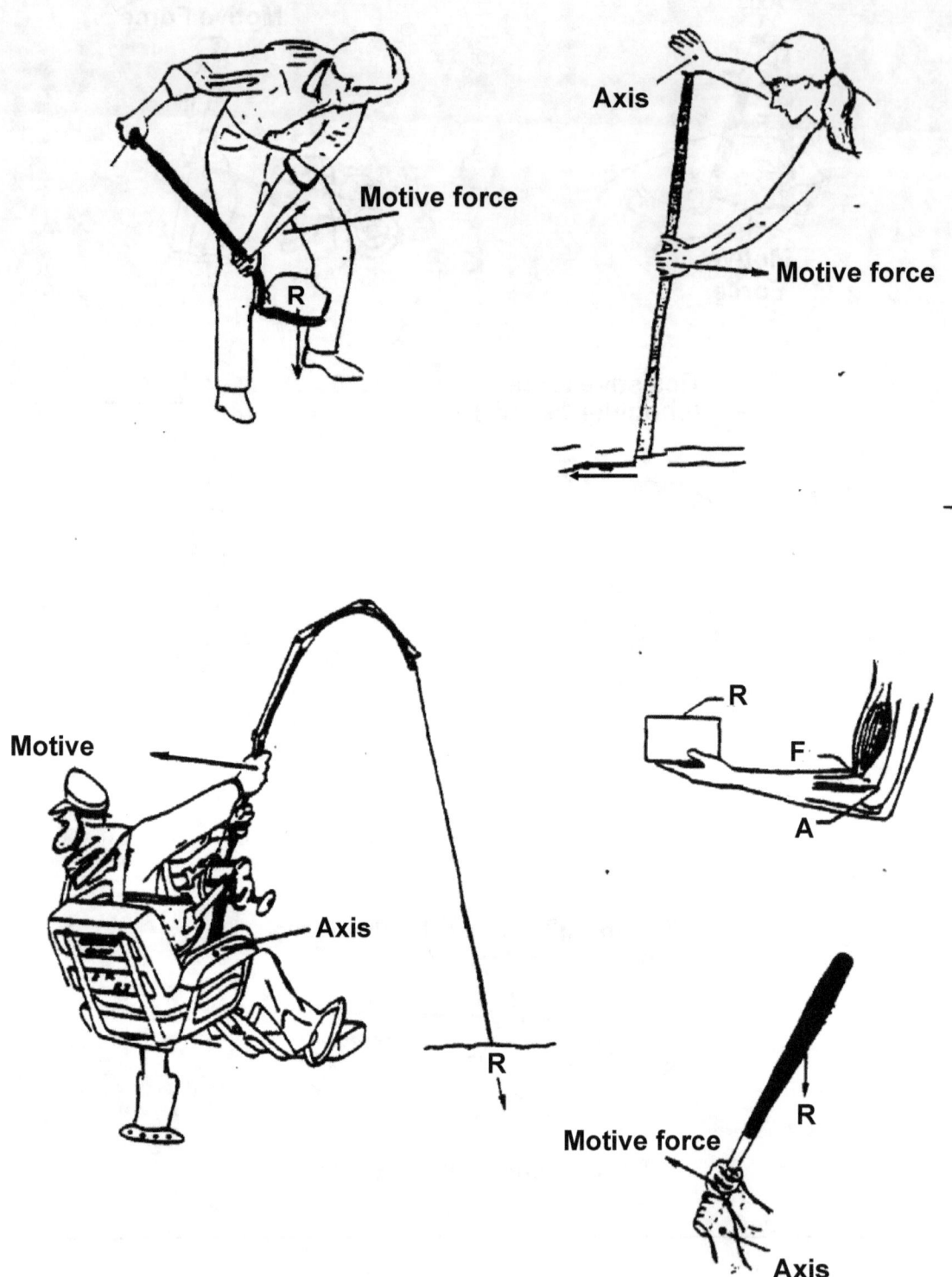

Muscle force is applied where muscles insert on bones. With a few exceptions, the body consists primarily of third-class levers, with bones functioning as the levers and contracting innervated muscles acting as the fulcrums or by gravity acting on various body masses. As a result, the human body favors speed and range of motion over force.

Because most human body levers are long, their distal ends can move rapidly. Thus, the body is capable of swift, wide movements at the expense of abundant muscle force.

The human body easily performs tasks involving rapid movement with light objects. Very heavy tasks require a device for the body to secure an advantage of force.

Sports instruments increase body levers, thereby increasing the speed of an object's imparting force. However, the use of sports instruments requires more muscle force.

The body's leverage rarely includes one part of the body (a simple, singular lever). Movement of the body is an outcome of a system of levers operating together. However, levers do function in sequence when the force produced by the system of levers is dependent on the speed at the extremity. Many levers function simultaneously for a heavy task (e.g. pushing).

APPLY MECHANICAL PRINCIPLES OF MOTION TO PHYSICAL EDUCATION ACTIVITIES

1. **Inertia** - tendency of a body or object to remain in its present state of motion; an object will stay in a prescribed straight path and will move at its given speed unless some force acts to change it.

2. **Projecting objects for vertical distance** - the forces of gravity and air resistance prevent vertically projected objects from continuing at their initial velocities. The downward, resistive force of gravity slows a projectile directed upward until it halts (at the peak of vertical path). At this point, the downward force of gravity becomes an incentive force that increases the speed of the object until it confronts another force (the earth or other external object) that slows the object until it stops. When the object stops ascending and begins to descend, gravity alters the object's direction of motion. Air resistance (of still air) always opposes the object's motion. Therefore, an ascending object's air resistance is downward and a descending object's air resistance is upward. An increase in velocity increases air-drag force that decreases the magnitude of the drag as the object moves upward, slowing in velocity. The magnitude of the drag increases as the object moves faster and faster downward.

Moreover, the direction and magnitude of the object's acceleration, due to the force of gravity, are constant while direction and magnitude of changes, due to air resistance, are dependent on the object's speed and direction.

An object travels the highest when projected with the greatest velocity, and the object's weight affects neither gravity's upward deceleration nor its downward acceleration. The object's weight, however, is a factor in calculating the net force acting on the object's vertical movement through the air.

- **Projecting the body for vertical distance** - for these activities (e.g. vertical leaping), the height of reach of the hand from the ground is the significant factor. The following three factors determine the body's reach height: 1) the center of gravity's vertical velocity, 2) the center of gravity's height from the ground at takeoff, and 3) the vertical distance of the fingertips relative to the center of gravity at the peak of the jump.

- **Projecting for vertical distance with a horizontal component** - for these activities (e.g. high jumping), a running approach to the point of takeoff produces horizontal velocity even with a 100% vertical takeoff.

- **Projecting for horizontal distance** - a body will continue to travel horizontally until an external force, usually the ground, halts it. Gravity stops vertical movement while ground friction eventually stops horizontal velocity, preventing any additional horizontal distance. "air time" increases when the initial upward vertical velocity component is greater. There is a tradeoff between maximum "air time" (determined by vertical velocity) and maximum horizontal distance (determined by horizontal velocity).

- **Horizontal projections with equal takeoff and landing heights** - maximum horizontal distance occurs if the projection angle is 45-degrees.

- **Horizontal projections with unequal takeoff and landing heights** – the height of an object's center of gravity depends on a performer's height and his/her location in relation to the ground upon release or impact of the object. The greater the object's travel time forward, the farther the object's distance before landing. Hence, a taller performer has an automatic advantage over a shorter performer who throws with the same projection velocity. In addition, the greater the difference between takeoff and landing heights, the smaller the optimum angle of release - given equal projection velocities.

Projecting objects for accuracy:

- **Vertical plane targets** - accuracy is easiest when using a trajectory that is perpendicular to the target as it coincides with the target face. As projection distance increases, a more curved parabolic path is required.

- **Horizontal plane targets** - the more vertically the projectile arrives at the target (as close to 90 degrees as possible), the greater the likelihood of successfully hitting the target and preventing the object from rolling or sliding away from the target area.

Projecting the body for accuracy - for moving or positioning the body (or its segments) to achieve an ideal/model performance by body maneuvers, the performer projects his/her center of gravity to an imaginary target point in space.

Projecting objects for accuracy when speed can enhance performance - the performer must increase the angle of projection for slower projection speeds (must consider participant's height).

- **Acceleration** - the movement response (acceleration) of a system depends not only on the net external force applied, but also depends on the resistance to movement change (inertia).

If an object's acceleration is proportional to the applied force, greater force produces greater acceleration. An object's acceleration is inversely proportional to its mass (the greater the mass, the less the acceleration).

- **Angular acceleration** (rate that an object's angular speed or direction changes) - angular acceleration is great when there is a large change in angular velocity in a short amount of time. A rigid body (or segment) encounters angular acceleration or deceleration only when a net external torque is applied. When torque stops, a new velocity is reached and maintained until another torque occurs. Acceleration is always in the direction of the acting torque, and the greater the torque, the greater the angular acceleration.

- **Linear acceleration** (time rate of change in velocity) - an object's magnitude of acceleration is significant if there is a large change of velocity in a small amount of time. When the same velocity changes over a longer period of time, acceleration is small. Acceleration occurs only when force is applied. When the force stops, the object/body reaches a new speed and the object/body continues at the new speed until a force changes that speed or direction. In addition, the direction of acceleration is the same direction as the applied net force. A large force produces a large acceleration. A small force produces a modest acceleration.

- **Zero/Constant Acceleration** (constant velocity) - there is no change in a system's velocity when the object/body moves at a given velocity and encounters equal, opposing forces. Hence, velocity is constant since no force causes acceleration or deceleration.

- **Acceleration caused by gravity** - a falling object/body continues to accelerate at the rate of 9.8 m/sec. (32 ft/sec.) throughout its fall.

- **Radial acceleration (direction change caused by centripetal force)** - centripetal force is aimed along an illusory line (the circular path) at any instant. Therefore, it is the force responsible for change of direction. The bigger the mass, the greater the centripetal force required. A tighter turn magnifies direction change (radial acceleration), so friction must increase to offset the increased acceleration. Maximum friction (centrifugal force) reduces speed. A combination of the variables mass, radius of curvature, speed of travel, and centripetal force cause radial acceleration.

Action/Reaction - every action has an equal and opposite reaction.

- **Linear motion** - the larger the mass, the more it resists motion change initiated by an outside force.

Body segments exert forces against surfaces they contact. These forces and the reaction of the surfaces result in body movement. For example, a runner propels himself forward by exerting a force on the ground (as long as the surface has sufficient friction and resistance to slipping). The force of the contact of the runner's foot with the ground and the equal and opposite reaction of the ground produces movement. Paddling a canoe or swimming exerts a backward force by pushing water backwards, causing a specific velocity that is dependent on the stroke's force - as well as the equal and opposite force made by the water pushing forward against the paddle moving the canoe forward or the swimmer's arm moving the swimmer forward.

Every torque (angular motion) exerted by one body/object on another has another torque equal in magnitude and opposite direction exerted by the second body/object on the first. Changing angular momentum requires a force that is equal and opposite of the change in momentum.

Performing actions in a standing position requires the counter pressure of the ground against the feet for accurate movement of one or more parts of the body.

SKILL 5.6 Identify strategies to develop correct skill performance.

RECOGNIZE ERRORS IN SKILL PERFORMANCE

Because performing a skill involves several components, determining why a participant is performing poorly may be difficult. Instructors may have to assess several components of a skill to determine the root cause of poor performance and appropriately correct errors. **An instructor should have the ability to identify performance errors by observing a student's mechanical principles of motion during the performance of a skill. Process assessment** is a subjective, observational approach to identifying errors in the form, style, or mechanics of a skill.

A strategy to help to correct skill performance is repetition. Assign a peer who has mastered the skill to work with one who does not. By working together and through repetition of the correct skill performance, the struggling student can overcome and develop the skill performance needed the majority of the time. With peers assisting them, the student's tend to be more motivated to develop the correct skill performance.

RECOGNIZE APPROPRIATE OBJECTIVE MEASUREMENTS OF FUNDAMENTAL SKILLS

Instructors should use **product assessments**, quantitative measures of a movement's end result, to evaluate fundamental skills objectively. Objective measurements such as: how far, how fast, how high, or how many are quantitative measures of product assessments.

A **criterion-referenced test** (superior to a standardized test) or a **standardized norm-referenced test** can provide valid and reliable data for objectively measuring fundamental skills.

USE SKILL ASSESSMENT INFORMATION TO IDENTIFY ERROR CORRECTION STRATEGIES

Instructors can use criterion-referenced standards to diagnose weaknesses and correct errors in skill performance because such performance standards define appropriate levels of achievement. Instructors can however, also use biomechanical instructional objectives. The following list describes the skill assessment criteria of several representative activities:

Archery - measuring accuracy in shooting a standardized target from a specified place.

Bowling - calculating the bowling average that is attained under standardized conditions.

Golf – assessing the score after several rounds.

Swimming - counting the number of breaststrokes needed in order to swim 25 yards.

Examples of error correction activities include reteaching the non-learned skills, breaking the skill down into individual parts and showing video's of the skill being performed correctly.

SKILL 5.7 Analyze the mechanics of a skill or sequence of movements and identify ways in which the performer can improve the performance.

When introducing new skills, physical education instructors should break the skill down into components and present the components sequentially, from easiest to most difficult. The following are patterns of sequential development for locomotor, nonlocomotor, and manipulative skills.

IDENTIFY SEQUENTIAL DEVELOPMENT AND ACTIVITIES FOR LOCOMOTOR SKILL ACQUISITION

Sequential Development of locomotor skills - crawl, creep, walk, run, jump, hop, gallop, slide, leap, skip, step-hop.

- **Activities to develop walking skills** include walking slower and faster in place; walking forward, backward, and sideways with slower and faster paces in straight, curving, and zigzag pathways with various lengths of steps; pausing between steps; and changing the height of the body.

- **Activities to develop running skills** include having students pretend they are playing basketball, trying to score a touchdown, trying to catch a bus, finishing a lengthy race, or running on a hot surface.

- **Activities to develop jumping skills** include alternating jumping with feet together and feet apart, taking off and landing on the balls of the feet, clicking the heels together while airborne, and landing with a foot forward and a foot backward.

- **Activities to develop galloping skills** include having students play a game of Fox and Hound, with the lead foot representing the fox and the back foot the hound trying to catch the fox (alternate the lead foot).

- **Activities to develop sliding skills** include having students hold hands in a circle and sliding in one direction, then sliding in the other direction.

- **Activities to develop hopping skills** include having students hop all the way around a hoop and hopping in and out of a hoop reversing direction. Students can also place ropes in straight lines and hop side-to-side over the rope from one end to the other and change (reverse) the direction.

- **Activities to develop skipping skills** include having students combine walking and hopping activities leading up to skipping.

- **Activities to develop step-hopping skills** include having students practice stepping and hopping activities while clapping hands to an uneven beat.

IDENTIFY SEQUENTIAL DEVELOPMENT AND ACTIVITIES FOR NONLOCOMOTOR SKILL ACQUISITION

Sequential Development of nonlocomotor skills: stretch, bend, sit, shake, turn, rock and sway, swing, twist, dodge, and fall.

Activities to develop stretching include lying on the back and stomach and stretching as far as possible; stretching as though one is reaching for a star, picking fruit off a tree, climbing a ladder, shooting a basketball, or placing an item on a high self; waking and yawning.

Activities to develop bending include touching knees and toes then straightening the entire body and straightening the body halfway; bending as though picking up a coin, tying shoes, picking flowers/vegetables, and petting animals of different sizes.

Activities to develop sitting include practicing sitting from standing, kneeling, and lying positions without the use of hands.

Activities to develop falling skills include first collapsing in one's own space and then pretending to fall like bowling pins, raindrops, snowflakes, a rag doll, or Humpty Dumpty.

IDENTIFY SEQUENTIAL DEVELOPMENT AND ACTIVITIES FOR MANIPULATIVE SKILL DEVELOPMENT

Sequential Development of manipulative skills: striking, throwing, kicking, ball rolling, volleying, bouncing, catching, and trapping.

Activities to develop striking begin with the striking of stationary objects by a participant in a stationary position. Next, the person remains still while trying to strike a moving object. Then, both the object and the participant are in motion as the participant attempts to strike the moving object.

Activities to develop throwing include throwing yarn/foam balls against a wall, then at a big target, and finally at targets decreasing in size.

Activities to develop kicking include alternating feet to kick balloons/beach balls, then kicking them under and over ropes. Change the type of ball as proficiency develops.

Activities to develop ball rolling include rolling different size balls to a wall, then to targets decreasing in size.

Activities to develop volleying include using a large balloon and, first, hitting it with both hands, then one hand (alternating hands), and then using different parts of the body. Change the object as students gain proficiency (balloon, to beach ball, to foam ball, etc.).

Activities to develop bouncing include starting with large balls and, first, using both hands to bounce, and then, using one hand (alternate hands).

Activities to develop catching include using various objects (balloons, beanbags, balls, etc.) to catch and, first, catching the object the participant has thrown him/herself, then catching objects someone else threw, and finally increasing the distance between the catcher and the thrower.

Activities to develop trapping include trapping slow and fast rolling balls; trapping balls (or other objects such as beanbags) that are lightly thrown at waist, chest, and stomach levels; trapping different size balls.

SKILL 5.8 Identify how components of skill-related fitness affect performance.

The skill-related components of physical fitness are **agility, balance, coordination, power, reaction time, and speed.** A student's natural, genetic abilities in these areas greatly affect performance in fitness and athletic activities. While heredity plays a major role in each student's ability level related to performing skill-related components, a strong knowledge and application of fundamentals, practice and coaching can improve performance.

The effect of factors such as gender, age, environment, nutrition, heredity and substance abuse is also crucial in understanding adolescent fitness performance. Girls mature earlier than boys do, but boys quickly catch up and grow larger and stronger. Age, combined with maturity level, influences a child's physical strength, flexibility, and coordination. Good nutrition positively influences the quality of a child's physical activity level, while poor nutrition has the opposite effect. Adverse environmental conditions such as high heat or poor air quality strongly affect activity level. Students that inherit favorable physical characteristics will perform better and with more ease than those who aren't so fortunate. Substance abuse of any sort – alcohol, tobacco, or drugs – is a detriment to physical performance.

Dealing with factors that are out of the teacher's control requires both structure and flexibility. When necessary, make adjustments amongst the students and/or the activity. For example, when teaching how to throw a softball, don't hesitate to pair girls with boys if their maturity and strength levels are similar. If the distance is too far for some pairs, move them closer.

If some pairs are more advanced, challenge them by increasing the partner's distance while continuing to work on accuracy and speed. Add a personal challenge to see how many times they can toss without dropping the ball. Finally, having more advanced students teach their peers that aren't as competent will benefit all students.

COMPETENCY 6.0   **KNOWLEDGE OF HEALTH AND WELLNESS AND ITS RELATIONSHIP TO PHYSICAL ACTIVITY**

SKILL 6.1   **Analyze health-related components of physical fitness.**

There are five health related components of physical fitness: **cardio-respiratory or cardiovascular endurance, muscle strength, muscle endurance, flexibility, and body composition.**

Cardiovascular endurance – the ability of the body to sustain aerobic activities (activities requiring oxygen utilization) for extended periods.

Muscle strength – the ability of muscle groups to contract and support a given amount of weight.

Muscle endurance – the ability of muscle groups to contract continually over a period of time and support a given amount of weight.

Flexibility – the ability of muscle groups to stretch and bend.

Body composition – an essential measure of health and fitness. The most important aspects of body composition are body fat percentage and ratio of body fat to muscle.

Wellness has two major components: understanding the basic human body functions and how to care for and maintain personal fitness, and developing an awareness and knowledge of how certain everyday factors, stresses, and personal decisions can affect one's health. Teaching fitness needs to go along with skill and activity instruction. Life-long fitness and the benefits of a healthy lifestyle need to be part of every P.E. teacher's curriculum. Teaching and teaching thematically with other subject matter in classrooms would be the ideal method to teach health to adolescents.

Incorporating wellness into the P.E. teacher's lesson plan doesn't need to take that much time or effort. For example, you can teach students to understand that if you put more calories in your body than what you burn, you will gain weight. Teaching nutrition and the caloric content of foods in P.E. can be as simple as learning the amount of calories burned when participating in different sports for a set amount of time.

A more sophisticated lesson on nutrition can have students understand the relationship between caloric intake and caloric expenditure. Students could keep a food diary, tabulating the caloric content of their own diets while comparing it to an exercise diary to track the calories they've burned.

Another example of incorporating wellness into the P.E. curriculum would be participation in endurance running activities. Having students run a set distance and then giving them a finish time rewards the faster students and defeats the slower students. In addition to a final time, teach students a more beneficial way of measuring one's cardiovascular fitness by understanding pulse rate.

Teach students how to take their own pulse, how pulse rates vary at different stages of exercise (i.e. resting pulse, target pulse, recovery pulse, etc.), how pulse rates can differ between boys and girls, and encourage them to keep track of their own figures. As students gather their data, whole group, teacher-led discussions about similarities, differences and patterns that are developing, would teach students how to effectively and easily monitor their own vital signs.

SKILL 6.2 Interpret data from physical fitness assessments for diagnosis and prescription.

Data from physical fitness assessments identify an individual's level of fitness and the components of fitness in need of improvement. We compare data to fitness standards and norms.

Cardio-respiratory data identifies an individual's functional aerobic capacity by the predicted maximum oxygen consumption. This can partially explain natural leanness, running ability, and motivation.

Muscle strength data identifies an individual's ability to execute some basic skills, an individual's potential for injury, an individual's potential to develop musculoskeletal problems, and an individual's potential to cope with life threatening situations.

Muscle strength data identifies an individual's ability to exercise continually for an extended period of time and an individual's potential for developing musculoskeletal problems.

Flexibility data identifies an individual's potential for motor skill performance, an individual's potential for developing musculoskeletal problems (including poor posture), and an individual's potential for performing activities of daily living.

Body composition is an indicator of an individual's health status and potential to participate in physical activities. Specifically, body composition addresses an individual's fat to muscle ratio.

The following is a list of tests that instructors can use to assess the physical fitness of students.

Cardio-respiratory fitness tests – maximal stress test, sub-maximal stress test, Bruce Protocol, Balke Protocol, Astrand and Rhyming Test, PWC Test, Bench Step Test, Rockport Walking Fitness Test, and Cooper 1.5 Mile Run/Walk Fitness Test.

Muscle strength tests – dynamometers (hand, back, and leg), cable tensiometer, The 1-RM Test (repetition maximum: bench press, standing press, arm curl, and leg press), bench-squat, sit-ups (one sit up holding a weight plate behind the neck), and lateral pull-down.

Muscle endurance tests – squat-thrusts, pull-ups, sit-ups, lateral pull-downs, bench presses, arm curls, push-ups, and dips.

Flexibility tests – sit and reach, Kraus-Webber Floor Touch Test, trunk extension, forward bend of trunk, Leighton Flexometer, shoulder rotation/flexion, and goniometer.

Body Composition determination – Hydrostatic Weighing, skin fold measurements, limb/girth circumference, and body mass index.

Agility tests – Illinois Agility Run.

Balance tests – Bass Test of Dynamic Balance (lengthwise and crosswise), Johnson Modification of the Bass Test of Dynamic Balance, modified sideward leap, and balance beam walk.

Coordination tests – Stick Test of Coordination.

Power tests – vertical jump.

Speed tests – 50-yard dash.

SKILL 6.3 Identify personal fitness programs that incorporate health-related components.

PHYSICAL FITNESS PROGRAMS INCORPORATING THE HEALTH-RELATED COMPONENTS TO MEET THE NEEDS OF STUDENTS

One domain in which self-assessment, problem-solving, and adjustments are of great importance is the development of fitness programs. Instructors can strive to design personal fitness programs that incorporate: mode, frequency, intensity, time, and progression.

The following is an example of a **cardio-respiratory fitness** program design:

- **Mode:** aerobic activities (e.g. walking, jogging, swimming, cycling, rowing).

- **Frequency:** 3 to 5 days/week.

- **Intensity:** 60% to 90% of maximum oxygen uptake or 60% to 80% target heart rate (THR).

- **Time:** 20 to 60 minutes of continuous or interval (non-continuous) activity (time depends on intensity level and fitness levels).

- **Progression:** instructor adjusts prescription according to an individual's fitness level and conditioning effects.

The following is an example of a **muscle strength** program design:

- **Mode:** weight training (isotonic/dynamic).

- **Frequency:** minimum 3 days/week to a maximum of every other day.

- **Intensity:** 60% to 90% of maximum muscle strength (1-RM).

- **Time:** 3 sets with 3 to 8 reps and a 60 second rest interval.

- **Progression:** increase workload (overload) when individual can perform 15 reps at 10 RM level.

The following is an example of a **muscle endurance** program design:

- **Mode:** weight training.

- **Frequency:** minimum 3 days/week up to every other day.

- **Intensity:** 30% to 60% of maximum muscle strength (1-RM).

- **Time:** 3 sets with 12 to 20 repetitions or until point of muscle fatigue with a 15 to 60 second rest interval.

- **Progression:** increase workload (overload) periodically based on number of continuous repetitions.

The following is an example of a **flexibility** program design:

- **Mode:** stretching.

- **Frequency:** 3 to 7 days/week.

- **Intensity:** just below individual's threshold of pain.

- **Time:** 3 sets with 3 repetitions holding stretches 15 to 30 seconds, with a 60 rest interval between sets.

The following is an example of a **body composition** program design:

- **Mode:** combining aerobic exercise and weight training and a moderate reduction of caloric intake.

- **Frequency:** minimum of 3 days/week; however, daily is best.

- **Intensity:** low intensity, long duration.

- **Time:** 45 to 60 minutes of aerobic activity; 3 sets with a minimum of 6 repetitions with weights every other day.

- **Progression:** periodically increase as individual improves.

SKILL 6.4 Identify components of nutrition.

The components of nutrition are **carbohydrates, proteins, fats, vitamins, minerals, and water.**

Carbohydrates – the main source of energy (glucose) in the human diet. The two types of carbohydrates are simple and complex. Complex carbohydrates have greater nutritional value because they take longer to digest, contain dietary fiber, and do not excessively elevate blood sugar levels. Common sources of carbohydrates are fruits, vegetables, grains, dairy products, and legumes.

Proteins – are necessary for growth, development, and cellular function. The body breaks down consumed protein into component amino acids for future use. Major sources of protein are meat, poultry, fish, legumes, eggs, dairy products, grains, and legumes.

Fats – a concentrated energy source and important component of the human body. The different types of fats are saturated, monounsaturated, and polyunsaturated. Polyunsaturated fats are the healthiest because they may lower cholesterol levels, while saturated fats increase cholesterol levels. Common sources of saturated fats include dairy products, meat, coconut oil, and palm oil. Common sources of unsaturated fats include nuts, most vegetable oils, and fish.

Vitamins and minerals – organic substances that the body requires in small quantities for proper functioning. People acquire vitamins and minerals in their diets and in supplements. Important vitamins include A, B, C, D, E, and K. Important minerals include calcium, phosphorus, magnesium, potassium, sodium, chlorine, and sulfur.

Water – makes up 55 – 75% of the human body. It is essential for most bodily functions. Water is obtained through foods and liquids.

DETERMINE THE ADEQUACY OF DIETS IN MEETING THE NUTRITIONAL NEEDS OF STUDENTS

Nutritional requirements *vary from person-to-person.* General guidelines for meeting adequate nutritional needs are: *no more than 30% total caloric intake from fats* (preferably 10% from saturated fats, 10% from monounsaturated fats, 10% from polyunsaturated fats), *no more than 15% total caloric intake from protein* (complete), *and at least 55% of caloric intake from carbohydrates* (mainly complex carbohydrates).

Exercise and diet help maintain proper body weight by equalizing caloric intake and caloric output.

RECOGNIZE FALLACIES AND DANGERS UNDERLYING SELECTED DIET PLANS

High Carbohydrate diets (i.e. Pritikin, Bloomingdale's) can produce rapid or gradual weight loss, depending on caloric intake. Vitamin and mineral supplements are usually needed because protein intake is low. These diets may or may not recommend exercising or permanent lifestyle changes, which are necessary to maintain one's weight.

High-Protein Diets promote the same myths, fallacies, and results as high carbohydrate diets. High-protein diets also require vitamin and mineral supplements. In addition, these diets are usually high in saturated fats and cholesterol because of the emphasis on meat products.

Liquid Formula Diets that are <u>physician/hospital run</u> (i.e. Medifast, Optifast ®) provide 800 or fewer calories a day consumed in liquid form. Dieters forgo food intake for 12 to 16 weeks in lieu of the protein supplement. Liquid diets require vitamin and mineral supplements and close medical supervision. Food is gradually reintroduced after the initial fast. These diets can result in severe and/or dangerous metabolic problems in addition to an irregular heartbeat, kidney infections and failure, hair loss, and sensations of feeling cold and/or cold intolerance. These diets are very expensive and have a high rate of failure.

Over-The-Counter Liquid Diets (i.e. Slimfast ®) are liquid/food bar supplements taken in place of one or more meals per day. Such diets advocate an intake of 1,000 calories daily. Carbohydrate, protein, vitamin, and mineral intake may be so low that the diet can be as dangerous as the medically supervised liquid diets when relied on for the only source of nutrition. Because of the lack of medical supervision, the side effects can be even more dangerous.

Over-The-Counter Diet Pills/Aids and Prescription Diet Pills (appetite suppressants) have as their main ingredient phenyl propanolamine hydrochloride [PPA]. Keeping weight off by using these products is difficult. Dizziness, sleeplessness, high blood pressure, palpitations, headaches, and tachycardia are potential side effects of these products. Moreover, prescription diet pills can be addictive.

Low Calorie Diets (caloric restricted) are the most misunderstood methods of weight loss. However, restricting the intake of calories is the way most people choose to lose weight. All the focus is on food, creating anxiety over the restriction of food - especially favorite foods. These diets are also difficult to maintain and have a high failure rate. Like the other diets, once the diet is over, dieters regain weight quickly because they fail to make permanent behavioral changes. Side effects of caloric restriction include diarrhea, constipation, Ketosis, a lower basal metabolic rate, blood-sugar imbalances, loss of lean body tissue, fatigue, weakness, and emotional problems. Dietary supplements are needed. Those who choose **fasting** (complete caloric restriction) to lose weight can deplete enough of the body's energy stores to cause death.

SKILL 6.5 Demonstrate knowledge of the relationship of nutrition and exercise in meeting the health needs of all students.

Nutrition and exercise are closely related concepts important to student health. An important responsibility of physical education instructors is to teach students about proper nutrition and exercise and how they relate to each other. The two key components of a healthy lifestyle are consumption of a balanced diet and regular physical activity. Nutrition absolutely plays an enormous role in physical performance. Proper nutrition produces high energy levels and allows for peak performance. Inadequate or improper nutrition can impair physical performance and lead to short-term and long-term health problems (e.g. depressed immune system and heart disease, respectively). Regular exercise improves overall health. Benefits of regular exercise include a stronger immune system, stronger muscles, bones, and joints, reduced risk of premature death, reduced risk of heart disease, improved psychological well-being, and weight management.

SKILL 6.6 Identify health risks that can be reduced by physical activity.

The following health risk factors improved by physical activity are: cholesterol levels, blood pressure, stress-related disorders, heart diseases, weight and obesity disorders, early death, certain types of cancer, musculoskeletal problems, mental health, and susceptibility to infectious diseases. The following is a list of physical activities that may reduce some of these health risks.

1. **Aerobic Dance**:
Health-related components of fitness = *cardio-respiratory, body composition.*
Skill-related components of fitness = *agility, coordination.*

2. **Bicycling**:
Health-related components of fitness = *cardio-respiratory, muscle strength, muscle endurance, body composition.*
Skill-related components of fitness = *balance.*

3. **Calisthenics:**
Health-related components of fitness = *cardio-respiratory, muscle strength, muscle endurance, flexibility, body composition.*
Skill-related components of fitness = *agility.*

4. **Circuit Training:**
Health-related components of fitness = *cardio-respiratory, muscle strength, muscle endurance, body composition.*
Skill-related components of fitness = *power.*

5. **Cross Country Skiing:**
Health-related component of fitness = *cardio-respiratory, muscle strength, muscle endurance, body composition.*
Skill-related components of fitness = *agility, coordination, power.*

6. **Jogging/Running:**
Health-related components of fitness = *cardio-respiratory, body composition.*

7. **Rope Jumping:**
Health-related components of fitness = *cardio-respiratory, body composition.*
Skill-related components of fitness = *agility, coordination, reaction time, speed.*

8. **Rowing:**
Health-related components of fitness = *cardio-respiratory, muscle strength, muscle endurance, body composition.*
Skill-related components of fitness = *agility, coordination, power.*

9. **Skating:**
Health-related components of fitness = *cardio-respiratory, body composition.*
Skill-related components of fitness = *agility, balance, coordination, speed.*

10. **Swimming/Water Exercises**:
Health-related components of fitness = *cardio-respiratory, muscle strength, muscle endurance, flexibility, body composition.*
Skill related components of fitness = *agility, coordination.*

11. **Walking (brisk):**
Health-related components of fitness = *cardio-respiratory, body composition.*

SKILL 6.7 Apply basic training principles and guidelines to improve physical fitness.

The **Overload Principle** is exercising at an above normal level to improve physical or physiological capacity (a higher than normal workload).

The **Specificity Principle** is overloading a particular fitness component. In order to improve a component of fitness, you must isolate and specifically work on a single component. Metabolic and physiological adaptations depend on the type of overload; hence, specific exercise produces specific adaptations, creating specific training effects.

The **Progression Principle** states that once the body adapts to the original load/stress, no further improvement of a component of fitness will occur without adding an additional load.

There is also a **Reversibility-of-Training Principle** in which all gains in fitness are lost with the discontinuance of a training program.

IDENTIFY WAYS IN WHICH WE CAN MODIFY OVERLOAD

We can modify overload by varying **frequency, intensity, and time**. Frequency is the number of times we implement a training program in a given period (e.g. three days per week). Intensity is the amount of effort put forth or the amount of stress placed on the body. Time is the duration of each training session.

COMPUTE THE TARGET HEART RATE ZONE

The target heart rate (THR) zone is a common measure of aerobic exercise intensity. Participants find their THR and attempt to raise their heart rate to the desired level for a certain period of time. There are three ways to calculate the target heart rate.

1. METs (maximum oxygen uptake), which is 60% to 90% of functional capacity.

2. Karvonean Formula = [Maximum heart rate (MHR) – Resting heart rate (RHR)] x intensity + RHR. MHR= 220 - Age
Intensity = Target Heart Range (which is 60% - 80% of MHR - RHR + RHR).
THR = (MHR - RHR) x .60 + RHR to (MHR - RHR) x .80 + RHR

3. Cooper's Formula to determine target heart range is:
THR = (220 - AGE) x .60 to (220 - AGE) x .80. **This is the most common used formula among physical educators.**

IDENTIFY HOW WE CAN IMPROVE THE HEALTH-RELATED COMPONENTS OF PHYSICAL FITNESS BY IMPLEMENTING THE PRINCIPLES OF OVERLOAD, PROGRESSION, AND SPECIFICITY

1. Cardio-respiratory Fitness

Overloading for cardio-respiratory fitness:

- **Frequency** = minimum of 3 days/week.
- **Intensity** = exercising in target heart-rate zone.
- **Time** = minimum of 20 minutes rate.

Progression for cardiovascular fitness:

- Begin at a frequency of 3 days/week and work up to no more than 6 days/week.
- Begin with an intensity near THR threshold and work up to 80% of THR.
- Begin at 20 minutes and work up to 60 minutes.

Specificity for cardiovascular fitness:

- To develop cardiovascular fitness, you must perform aerobic (with oxygen) activities for at least twenty minutes without developing an oxygen debt. Aerobic activities include, but are not limited to brisk walking, jogging, bicycling, and swimming.

2. Muscle Strength:

Overloading for muscle strength:

- **Frequency** = every other day
- **Intensity** = 60% to 90% of assessed muscle strength
- **Time** = 3 sets of 3 - 8 reps (high resistance with a low number of repetitions)

Progression for muscle strength:

- begin 3 days/week and work up to every other day
- begin near 60% of determined muscle strength and work up to no more than 90% of muscle strength

- begin with 1 set with 3 reps and work up to 3 sets with 8 reps

Specificity for muscle strength:

- to increase muscle strength for a specific part(s) of the body, you must target that/those part(s) of the body

3. Muscle endurance:

Overloading for muscle endurance:

- **Frequency** = every other day.

- **Intensity** = 30% to 60% of assessed muscle strength.

- **Time** = 3 sets of 12 - 20 reps (low resistance with a high number of reps).

Progression for muscle endurance:

- Begin 3 days/week and work up to every other day.

- Begin at 20% to 30% of muscle strength and work up to no more than 60% of muscle strength.

- Begin with 1 set with 12 reps and work up to 3 sets with 20 reps.

Specificity for muscle endurance:

- The same as for muscle strength.

4. Flexibility:

Overloading for flexibility:

- **Frequency**: 3 to 7 days/week.

- **Intensity**: stretch muscle beyond its normal length.

- **Time**: 3 sets of 3 reps holding stretch 15 to 60 seconds.

Progression for flexibility:

- Begin 3 days/week and work up to every day.

- Begin stretching with slow movement as far as possible without pain, holding at the end of the range of motion (ROM) and work up to stretching no more than 10% beyond the normal ROM.

- Begin with 1 set with 1 rep, holding stretches 15 seconds, and work up to 3 sets with 3 reps, holding stretches for 60 seconds.

Specificity for flexibility:

- ROM is joint specific.

5. Body composition:

Overloading to improve body composition:

- **Frequency**: daily aerobic exercise.

- **Intensity**: low.

- **Time**: approximately one hour.

Progression to improve body composition:

- Begin daily.

- Begin a low aerobic intensity and work up to a longer duration (see cardio-respiratory progression).

- Begin low-intensity aerobic exercise for 30 minutes and work up to 60 minutes of exercise.

Specificity to improve body composition:

- Increase aerobic exercise and decrease caloric intake.

IDENTIFY THE TECHNIQUES AND BENEFITS OF WARMING UP AND COOLING DOWN

Warming up is a gradual 5 to 10 minute aerobic warm-up in which the participant uses the muscles needed in the activity to follow (similar movements at a lower intensity). Warm-ups also include the stretching major muscle groups after a gradual warm-up.

The benefits of warming up are:

- Preparing the body for physical activity.
- Reducing the risk of musculoskeletal injuries.
- Releasing oxygen from myoglobin.
- Warming the body's inner core.
- Increasing the reaction of muscles.
- Bringing the heart rate to an aerobic conditioning level.

Cooling down is similar to warming up— a moderate to light tapering-off of vigorous activity at the end of an exercise session.

The benefits of cooling down are:

- Redistributing blood throughout the body to prevent pooling.
- Preventing dizziness.
- Facilitating the removal of lactic acid.

TEACHER CERTIFICATION STUDY GUIDE

SKILL 6.8 Identify exercises that benefit the major muscle groups of the body.

Some of the major muscle groups of the body important to physical fitness are the traps, delts, pecs, lats, obliques, abs, biceps, quadriceps, hamstrings, adductors, triceps, biceps, and glutes.

Dumbbell Shoulder Shrug
(Trapezius)

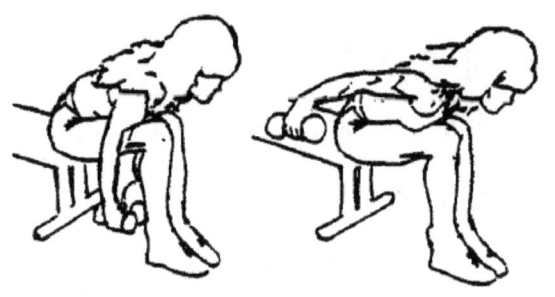

Seated Bent-Over Rear Deltoid Raise
(Rear Deltoids)

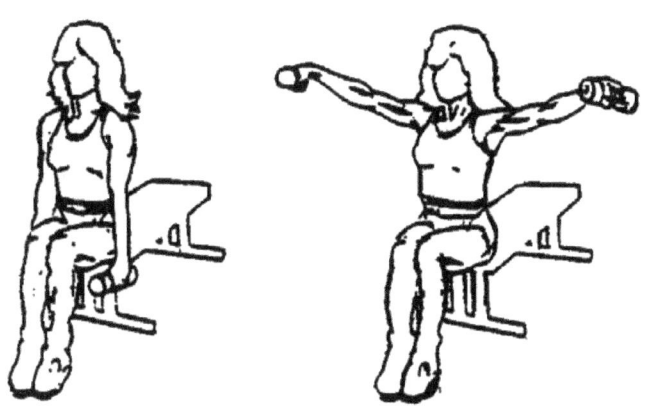

Seated Side Lateral Raise
(Front and Outer Deltoids)

TEACHER CERTIFICATION STUDY GUIDE

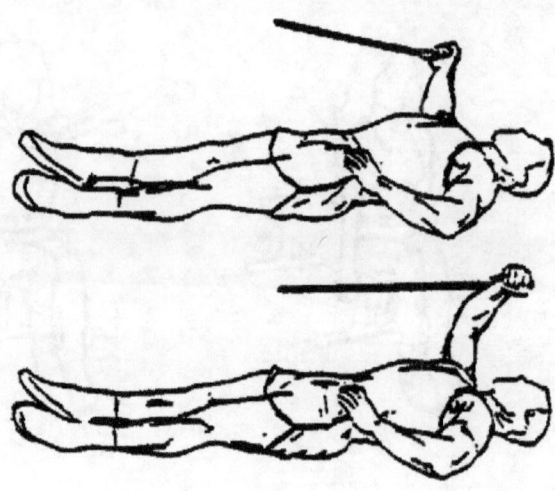

Lying Low-Pulley One-Arm Chest
(Lateral Pectorals)

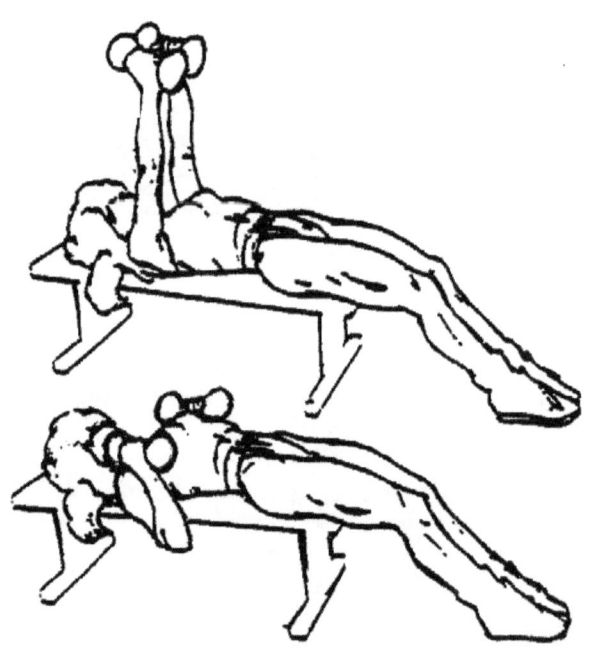

Flat Dumbbell Press
(Pectorals)

Medium-Grip Front-to-Rear Lat Pull Down
(Lats)

Straight-Arm Close-Grip Lat Pull Down
(Lats)

Dumbbell Side Bend
(Obliques)

Seated Barbell Twist
(Obliques)

Leg Pull-In
(Lower Abdominals)

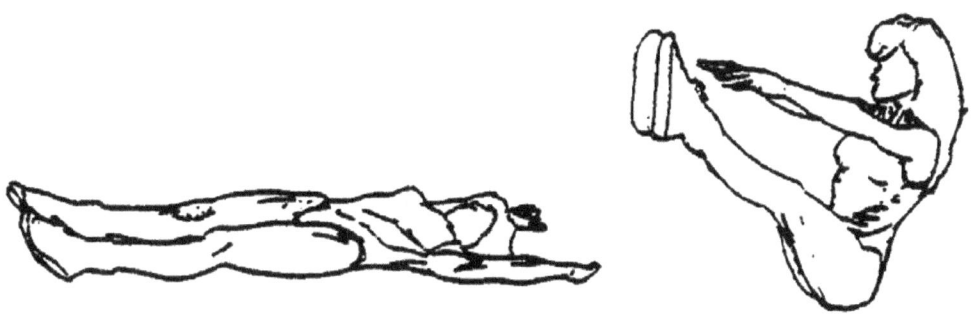

Jackknife Sit-Up
(Upper and Lower Abdominals)

Standing Alternated Dumbbell Curl
(Biceps)

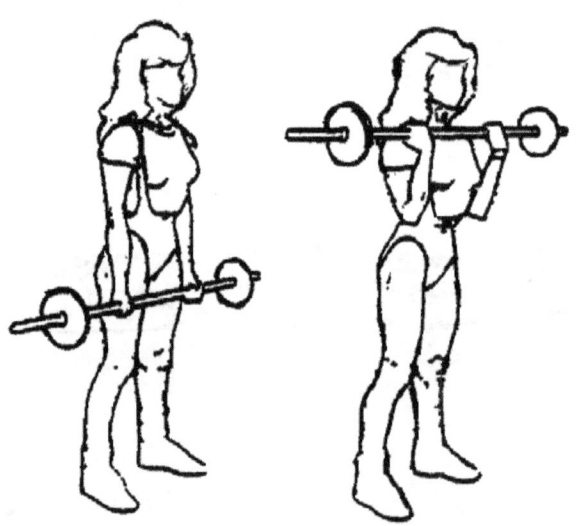

Standing Medium-Grip Barbell Curl
(Biceps)

Standing Close-Grip Easy-Curl-Bar Triceps Curl
(Triceps)

Standing Bent-Over One-Arm-Dumbbell Triceps Extension
(Triceps)

Flat-Footed Medium-Stance Barbell Half-Squat
(Thighs)

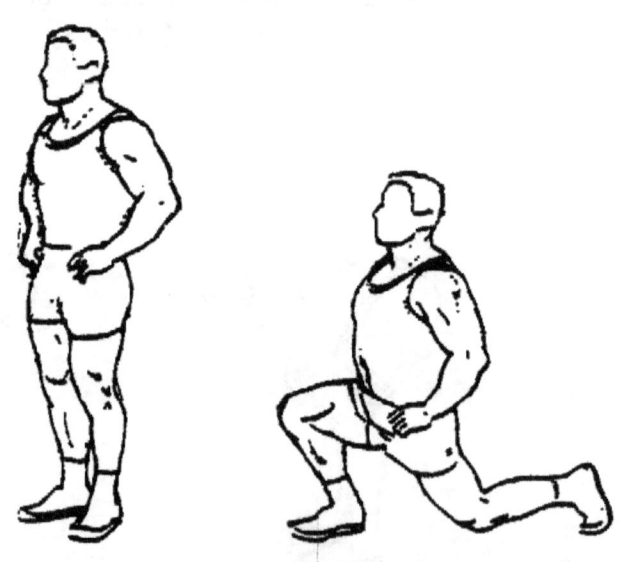

Freehand Front Lunge
(Thighs and Hamstrings)

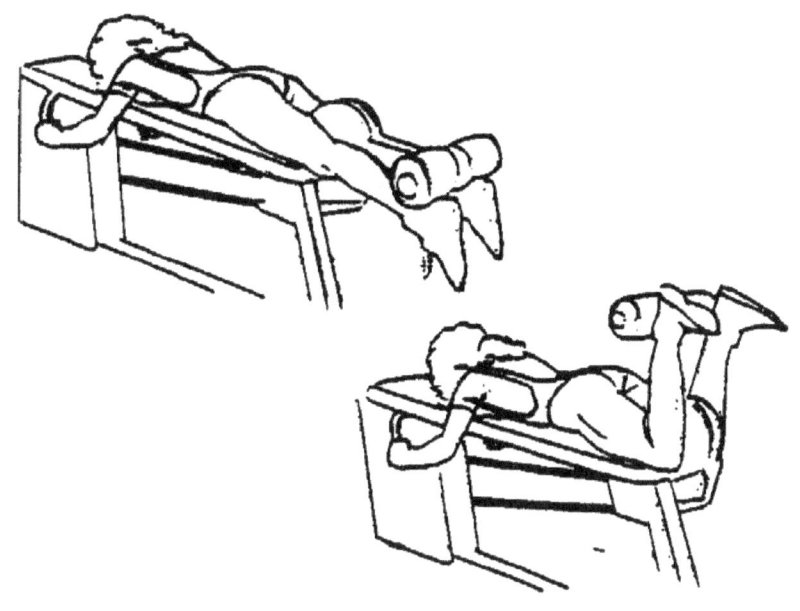

Thigh Biceps Curl on Leg Extension Machine
(Hamstrings)

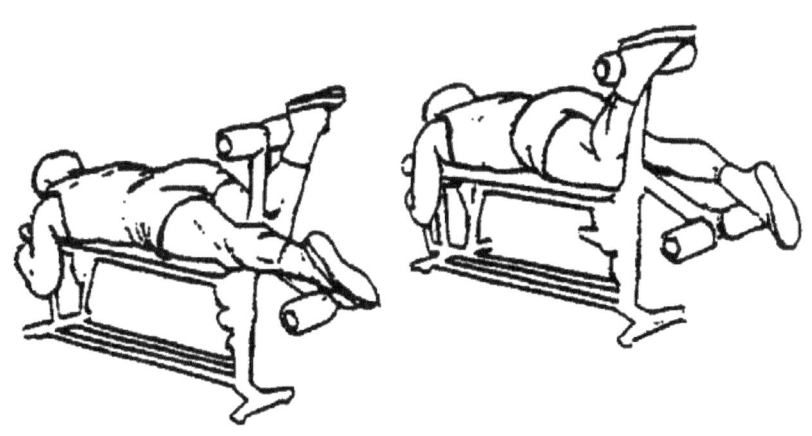

One-at-a-Time Biceps Curl on Leg Extension Machine
(Hamstrings)

Hip Abduction
(Hips)

Hip Adduction
(Inner Thigh)

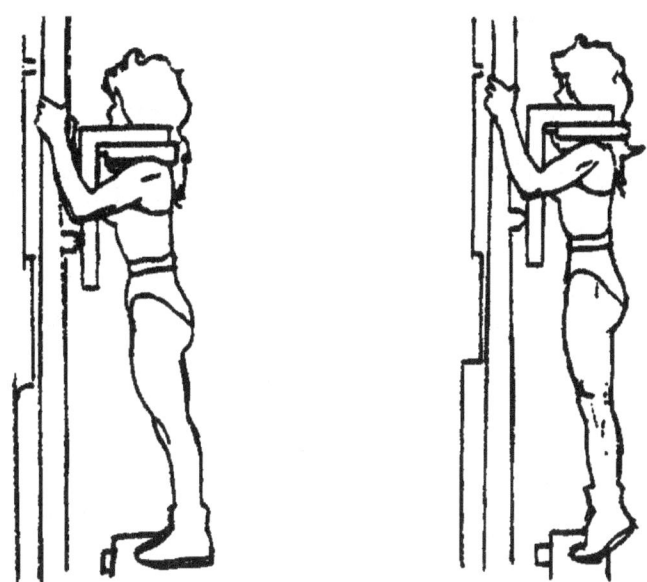

Standing Toe Raise on Wall Calf Machine
(Main Calf Muscles)

Standing Barbell Toe Raise
(Main Calf Muscles)

TEACHER CERTIFICATION STUDY GUIDE

Hip Extension
(Hips and Thighs)

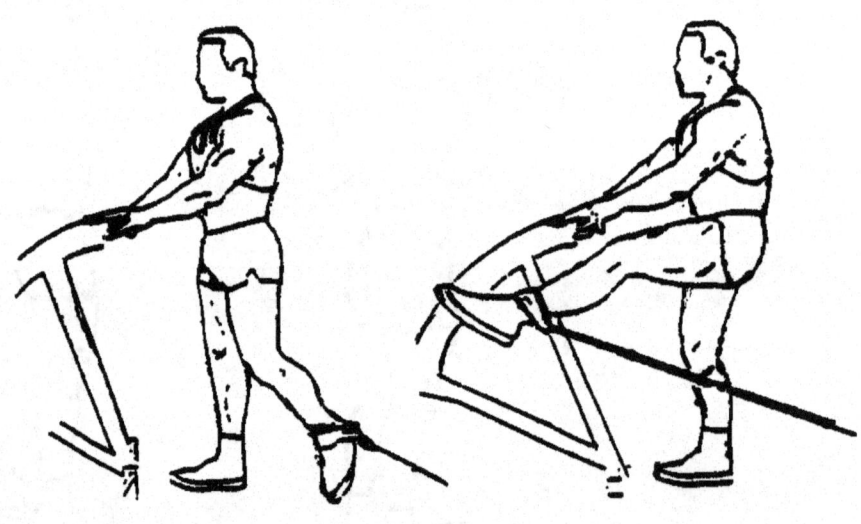

Hip Flexion
(Hip Flexors)

SKILL 6.9 Identify how the structure and function of the human body adapt to physical activity.

The structure and function of the human body adapts greatly to physical activity and exertion. How quickly the body adapts depends on a number of factors. Age, past history and experience in athletic and fitness activities, level of body composition and current health issues all play into the body's adaptation to physical activity. When challenged with any physical task, the human body responds through a series of integrated changes in function that involve most, if not all, of its physiological systems. Movement requires activation and control of the musculoskeletal system. The cardiovascular and respiratory systems provide the ability to sustain this movement over extended periods. When the body engages in exercise training several times, each of these physiological systems undergoes specific adaptations that increase the body's efficiency and capacity.

When the body works, it makes great demands on every muscle of the body. Either the muscles have to 'shut down' or they have to do work. The heart beats faster during strenuous exercise so that it can pump more blood to the muscles, and the stomach shuts down during strenuous exercise so that it does not waste energy that the muscles need. Exercising makes the muscles work like motors that use up energy in order to generate force. Muscles, also known as "biochemical motors," use the chemical adenosine triphosphate (ATP) as an energy source.

Different types of systems, such as the glycogen-lactic acid system, help muscles perform. Such systems help in producing ATP, which is extremely vital to working muscles. Aerobic respiration, which also helps in releasing ATP, uses the fatty acids from fat reserves in muscle and helps produce ATP for a much longer period of time.

The following points summarize the process of bodily adaptation to exercise:

• Muscle cells use the ATP they have floating around in about 3 seconds.
• The phosphagen system kicks in and supplies energy for 8 to 10 seconds.
• If exercise continues longer, the glycogen-lactic acid system kicks in.
• Finally, if exercise continues longer, aerobic respiration takes over. This would occur in endurance events such as an 800-meter dash, a marathon run, rowing, cross-country skiing, or distance skating.

Physical activity affects the cardiovascular and musculoskeletal systems the most. However, it also helps in proper functioning of metabolic, endocrine, and immune systems.

SKILL 6.10 Identify the physiological, psychological, and sociological benefits of physical activity.

Physiological benefits of physical activity include:

- Improved cardio-respiratory fitness.
- Improved muscle strength.
- Improved muscle endurance.
- Improved flexibility.
- More lean muscle mass and less body fat.
- Quicker rate of recovery.
- Improved ability of the body to utilize oxygen.
- Lower resting heart rate.
- Increased cardiac output.
- Improved venous return and peripheral circulation.
- Reduced risk of musculoskeletal injuries.
- Lower cholesterol levels.
- Increased bone mass.
- Cardiac hypertrophy and size and strength of blood vessels.
- Increased number of red cells.
- Improved blood-sugar regulation.
- Improved efficiency of thyroid gland.
- Improved energy regulation.
- Increased life expectancy.

Psychological benefits of physical activity include:

- Relief of stress.
- Improved mental health via better physical health.

- Reduced mental tension (relief from depression, improvement of sleeping patterns).

- Increased resistance to fatigue.

- Improved quality of life.

- Increased enjoyment of leisure time.

- Better capability to handle some stressors.

- Opportunity for successful experiences.

- Improved self-concept and self confidence.

- Better ability to recognize and accept limitations

- Improved appearance and sense of well-being.

- Better ability to meet challenges.

- Better sense of accomplishment.

Sociological benefits of physical activity include:

- The opportunity to spend time with family and friends and to meet new people and make new friends.

- The opportunity to be part of a team.

- The opportunity to participate in competitive experiences.

- The opportunity to experience the thrill of victory.

SKILL 6.11 Identify the contributions that physical education makes to lifelong physical activity and wellness.

The goal of physical education is to impart the knowledge, skills, and confidence necessary for students to enjoy a life of healthful physical activity. There are six standards for physical education:

- **Standard 1:** Demonstrates competency in motor skills and movement patterns needed to perform a variety of physical activities.

- **Standard 2:** Demonstrates understanding of movement concepts, principles, strategies, and tactics as they apply to the learning and performance of physical activities.

- **Standard 3:** Participates regularly in physical activity.

- **Standard 4:** Achieves and maintains a health-enhancing level of physical fitness.

- **Standard 5:** Exhibits responsible personal and social behavior that respects self and others in physical activity settings.

- **Standard 6:** Values physical activity for health, enjoyment, challenge, self-expression, and/or social interaction.

(source: National Association for Sport & Physical Education)

A comprehensive physical education curriculum emphasizes the importance of physical activity and nutrition to lifelong wellness. In addition, physical education should introduce students to various activities that promote healthy living. Finally, physical education should provide students with strategies to maintain proper nutrition and activity and design personal fitness programs.

SKILL 6.12 Identify community resources that promote lifelong physical activity and wellness.

Physical education instructors should research community resources that promote physical activity and wellness so they can better educate their students. One important group of community health resources are health organizations. For example, the American Heart Association can provide CPR certification training classes for students. Other important community health resources are fitness and sport clubs and leagues. Instructors should acquaint students with fitness clubs that allow people of all ages to remain physically active. In addition, physical education instructors should encourage students to join local sports clubs and leagues. Clubs, such as the Boys and Girls Club and the YMCA, provide structured recreational and physical activities. Local athletic leagues provide students with opportunities to participate in physical activities outside of school. This gives them experiences to develop skills in both competitive and cooperative environments.

COMPETENCY 7.0 KNOWLEDGE OF PRINCIPLES OF SOCIAL AND EMOTIONAL DEVELOPMENT THROUGH PHYSICAL ACTIVITY

SKILL 7.1 Identify the role physical activity can play in developing an understanding of diversity and cultural differences among people.

Physical activity and related games can introduce children to the concepts of equity and fairness. In addition, physical activity provides a venue for the interaction of diverse groups of people, allowing participants to observe and appreciate cultural differences and similarities.

- **Human Growth and Development** – Movement activities promote personal growth and development physically, by stimulating muscular development, and emotionally, by raising personal confidence levels among children, and by allowing them to explore concepts of inter-group equity that may at first seem threatening. To the insecure child, the concept that another group may be equal to his own may seem to diminish his group, and the child by extension.

- **Psychology** – Observation and interaction with the behavior of children from diverse backgrounds in a training environment (when the training activities tend to focus more on "doing," which feels more genuine to children than the classroom setting) allows the child to see in others the same sorts of behavioral reasoning processes that he sees in himself. This humanizes others from different backgrounds, and promotes concepts of equity among diverse groups.

- **Aesthetics** – Human movement activities create an opportunity for individual participation in activities with intrinsic aesthetic qualities. A gymnastic technique or a perfectly executed swing of a baseball bat relies on both physical training and a level of intuitive action. This is an artistic form of expression that is readily accessible to children. Recognizing beauty in the activities and performances of others (in some cases from groups different from that of the observer) is a humanizing experience.

SKILL 7.2 Identify the role physical activity plays in developing affective skills.

Physical activity can influence the development of affective skills both positively and negatively. Thus, physical education instructors must create an environment that maximizes the benefits of physical activity and minimizes the potential negative aspects.

Positive Individual Influences:

Feeling better; reduction of tension and depression; means of affiliation with others; exhilarating experiences; aesthetic experiences; positive body image; controls aggression, provides relaxation and a change of pace from long hours of work, study, or other stresses; provides challenge and sense of accomplishment; provides a way to be healthy and fit; improves self-esteem by mastering skills; provides creative experiences; positive addiction to exercise in contrast to negative substances.

Positive Group Influences of Physical Activity:

Cooperation; acceptance of all persons regardless of race, creed or origin; respect for others; assimilation of the group attitude; encouragement to develop a relationship of self to a group; development of a spirit of fairness; development of traits of good citizenship; development of leadership and following qualities; self-discipline; additional avenues for social acquaintances; social poise and self-understanding; social consciousness with an accompanying sense of values; and individual and social development.

Negative influences of Physical Activity:

Ego-centered athletes; winning at all costs; false values; harmful pressures; loss of identity; role conflict; aggression and violence; compulsiveness; over-competitiveness; addiction to exercise, when commitment to exercise has a higher priority than commitment to family and interpersonal relationships, work, and medical advice; escape or avoidance of problems; exacerbation of anorexia nervosa; exercise deprivation effects; fatigue; overexertion; poor eating habits; self-centeredness; preoccupation with fitness, diet, and body image.

COMPETENCY 8.0 KNOWLEDGE OF DEVELOPMENTALLY APPROPRIATE ASSESSMENT

SKILL 8.1 Identify assessment techniques, including authentic and traditional methods, for appropriate use within the cognitive domain.

IDENTIFY METHODS OF EVALUATION IN THE COGNITIVE DOMAIN OF LEARNING

1. **Standardized Tests** – scientifically constructed test with established validity and reliability.

2. **Teacher-made Tests** – developed personally by the teacher.

3. **Essay Tests/Written Assignments** – tests the ability to organize information presented logically in written paragraphs.

4. **Objective Tests** – true/false, multiple choice, matching, diagrams, completion, or short written response.

5. **Norm-Referenced Tests** – compares individual's score to those of others.

6. **Criterion-Referenced Tests** – Interpreting a score by comparing it to a predetermined standard.

SKILL 8.2 Identify assessment techniques, including authentic and traditional methods, for appropriate use within the affective domain.

The affective domain includes interests, appreciations, attitudes, values, and adjustments inherent in the acquisition of physical activities. To measure in the affective domain, the teacher can observe the student and keep a related anecdotal record. Alternatively, the instructor can use opinion polls or surveys. To measure the social progress of an individual, use a sociogram. It plots the associations an individual student has with his peers.

The following is a list of some appropriate tools available for the assessment of affective development.

SOCIAL MEASURES (behavior, leadership, acceptance, and personality/character):

- **Harrocks Prosocial Behavior Inventory** (HPBBI) – measures prosocial play behavior of 5th and 6th graders in recreational play.

- **Adams Prosocial Inventory** – measures high school students' prosocial behaviors in physical education classes.

- **Nelson Leadership Questionnaire** – determines leaders as perceived by instructors, coaches, classmates, and teammates.

- **Cowell Personal Distance Scale** – measures congruity of a student within a group and his/her yearly development.

- **Blanchard Behavior Rating Scale** – measures student personality and character.

ATTITUDE MEASURES (predisposition to certain actions):

- **McKethan Student Attitude Inventory-Instructional Processes in Secondary Physical Education** (SAI-IPSPE) – measures attitudes of students toward instructional processes (e.g. teacher's verbal behavior, nature of activities, patterns of class organization, and regulations and policies in conceptual physical education environment).

- **Toulmin Elementary Physical Education Attitude Scale** (TEPEAS) – measures attitudes of the physical education program of elementary school students.

- **Feelings About Physical Activity** – measures commitment to activity.

- **Children's Attitudes Toward Physical Activity-Revised** (CATPA) – measures significance students place on physical activity.

- **Willis Sports Attitudes Inventory - Form C** - measures motives of competition in sports (achievement, power, success, avoiding failure).

- **Sport Orientation Questionnaire - Form B** - measures behaviors of achievement and competition during exercising and sports.

- **McMahan Sportsmanship Questionnaire** – measures high school students' attitudes toward sportsmanship.

- **Physical Estimation and Attraction Scale** – measures motivation and measures interest.

SELF-CONCEPT MEASURES (self-perception):

- **Cratly Adaptation of Piers-Harris Self-Concept and Scale** – measures/estimates students' own feelings about their appearance and skill performance abilities.

- **Merkley Measure of Actual Physical Self** – measures perception of physical self relating to exercise and activity.

- **Nelson-Allen Movement Satisfaction** – measures satisfaction of movement.

- **Tanner Movement Satisfaction Scale** – measures students' own level of satisfaction/dissatisfaction with their own movement.

STRESS AND ANXIETY:

- **Stress Inventory** (Miller and Allen) – measures level of stress according to stress indicators.

- **Sport Competition Anxiety Tests** – measures anxiety toward competition via one's perception of the competition as threatening or non-threatening.

SKILL 8.3   Identify assessment techniques, including authentic and traditional methods, for appropriate use within the psychomotor domain.

A. GENERAL SKILLS:

1. **Iowa Brace Test** – measures motor educability.

2. **AAHPERD Youth Fitness Test** – measures motor capacity.

3. **AAHPERD Health Related Physical Fitness Test** – measures physical capacity.

4. **McCloy's General Motor Ability and Capacity Test** – measures motor ability and motor efficiency.

5. **Rodgers Strength Test** – measures muscular strength.

6. **Texas PE Test** – measures motor ability.

7. **Skills tests for accuracy** – involve kicking, throwing, or striking an object toward a goal; activities include volleyball serves, basketball free throws, badminton short serves, and basketball passing (e.g. AAHPERD: Basketball Passing Test for Accuracy).

8. **Skills test for total bodily movement** – requires performing a test course that involves movements similar to a given sport (e.g. AAHPERD: Basketball Control Test).

9. **Wall Volley Test** - measures the number of consecutive successful time/trials to pass, kick, throw, or strike an object at a wall in a given time (e.g. AAHPERD: Basketball Passing Test).

10. **Skills Tests for Power or Distance** - involve kicks, throws, or strokes to measure the ability to kick, throw, or strike an object (e.g. Badminton Drive for Distance and the Cornish Handball Power Test).

11. **Combination Tests** - composed of previous groupings to assess speed and accuracy.

B. TEACHER RATINGS – instructors create a numerical scale from one to five and rank performance based on specific, observable movements. An example is evaluating the use of space, use of focus, and variety of movements in a creative movement class.

C. STUDENT PROGRESS – score improvements (e.g. archery, badminton) and charting (e.g. basketball shots missed).

Instructors can administer skills tests for specific sports in one of two ways. First, rate individual performance based on a specified number of trials. Alternatively, evaluate skills using norm-referenced scales for a specific grade level.

Two problems with skill tests are that they take too much time to administer and their reliability is suspect.

SKILL 8.4   Select appropriate assessment strategies for curriculum design, lesson planning, student prescription, and program evaluation.

The trend in physical education assessment is to move increasingly away from norm- and criterion-referenced evaluations (i.e. measuring a student's achievements against the achievements of a normative group or against criteria that are arbitrarily set by either the educator or the governing educational body), and towards performance-based, or "authentic" evaluations. This creates difficulty for physical educators because it eliminates preset reference points.

The advantage of performance-based evaluations is they are equally fair to individuals with diverse backgrounds, special needs, and disabilities. In all cases, the instructor evaluates students based on their personal performance.

Portfolio construction is one way of assessing the performance of a student. The student chooses the achievements to add to the portfolio. This creates a tool that assesses current abilities and serves as a benchmark against which the instructor can measure future performance (thus evaluating progress over time, and not just a localized achievement).

Student self-assessment is often an important part of portfolios. The instructor should ask children questions like, "Where am I now? Where am I trying to go? What am I trying to achieve? How can I get from here to there?" This type of questioning involves the child more deeply in the learning process.

TYPES OF EVALUATION

Summative evaluation strategies involve assigning the student a letter or number grade, which can reflect both the student's performance and progress. Examples include:

- **Performance evaluations** – the instructor assigns a letter or number grade based on the student's performance on a task or set of tasks (e.g. push-ups and sit-ups, time to run one mile, etc.).

- **Progress evaluations** – the instructor assigns a letter or number grade based on the student's improvement in the ability to perform a task or set of tasks.

- **Effort evaluations** – the instructor assigns a letter or number grade based on the student's effort in working towards training goals.

- **Behavior evaluations** – the instructor assigns a letter or number grade based on the student's behavior in and attitude towards training and the training environment.

Formative evaluation strategies do not provide a letter or number grade to the student, but rather focus on a textual analysis of the student's performance and progress. Examples include a written analysis of the student's performance, progress, effort, attitude, and behavior.

APPLY STUDENT AND PROGRAM EVALUATIONS TO REDESIGNING INSTRUCTIONAL STRATEGIES IN PHYSICAL EDUCATION

The **Cheffers Adaptation of the Flanders Interaction Analysis System** (CAFAIS) and the **Academic Learning Time in Physical Education** (ALT-PE) are *Systematic Analyses* that detect continuous and discrete behaviors, actions and interactions, and teaching characteristics. Relating the goals of a systematic analysis to the data obtained during the instructional process can indicate which of the following instructional strategies need to changing:

- The ability of the teacher to question and the time engaged in questioning.

- The cognitive response of students.

- The time spent on task instruction (rate per minute).

- The number of times task instruction takes place (rate of occurrence).

Instructors can use the following **Systematic Observational Evaluations** to identify changes that need to be made in events, in duration, in groups, and in self recording:

- **Event Recording** (rate-per-minute, rate of occurrence) – counts the number of attempts students have to try a skill and the number of positive teacher-student interactions.

- **Duration Recording** – measures amount of time teacher spends on instructions, time spent on managing student activities, and time spent managing the participation of students.

- **Group Time Sampling/Playcheck Recording** – counts the number of students participating in the activity.

- **Self Recording** – students sign in their arrival time to class and how many completed tasks they accomplish.

Student assessments that can facilitate changes in instructional strategies include:

- **Formal assessments** such as win/loss records, written tests, skills tests, performance records, and reviewing videotaped performances.

- **Informal assessments** such as rating scales, observational performance descriptions, completing skills checklist, and utilizing observational time.

SKILL 8.5 **Interpret results of assessment for curriculum design, lesson planning, student prescription, and program evaluation.**

Instructors should compare assessment data to grade equivalency norms to determine where each student is relative to where he should be. However, the instructor should place the most emphasis on evaluating the student relative to past performance. Progress is more important than current achievement. A learning-disabled student might display below average levels of achievement despite having made a great deal of progress, while a gifted student might be above grade equivalency norms despite stagnation.

Instructors should communicate assessment data differently to students, parents, and school board members.

- **Assessment data communicated to students** should be encouraging, and should be limited to a textual analysis of the student's progress and effort (it is not helpful or encouraging to remind a student that he/she is below grade level norms, especially if he/she has worked hard and made progress). The ultimate purpose of assessment data communicated to a student is to encourage continue to improve and work hard.

TEACHER CERTIFICATION STUDY GUIDE

- **Assessment data communicated to parents** should also be encouraging and should focus on the student's progress and effort.

  That being said, it is also important that a parent receive an accurate picture of the student's status relative to grade-level norms, especially if the child is in need of remedial assistance.

- **Assessment data communicated to school board members** is generally more summative in nature (a letter or number grade) and is uniformly spelled out in the way of school district forms. Since school board members will generally see evaluations of entire classes at a time without knowing the individual students, it is not important for them to receive an encouraging picture of an individual student's progress. It is more important for them to see both current achievement levels and rates of progress to properly assess curriculum design, lesson planning, and program evaluation. Again, this information is found on pertinent forms maintained in each school office, provided by individual school districts.

SKILL 8.6 Select methods of assessment appropriate for an inclusive environment.

(*See Skill 8.4*)

Inclusion describes the attempt to accommodate all students in the learning process. An inclusive learning environment follows the principle that all students are full members of the school community and, thus, should have equal opportunities to learn and achieve success. Inclusive physical education classrooms meet the needs of students of varying ability levels and developmental stages, ethnic and socioeconomic backgrounds, and those students with physical and mental disabilities. Appropriate assessment techniques for an inclusive educational environment include self-assessments, formative assessments, informal assessments, and assessments that evaluate effort and progress rather than end results.

COMPETENCY 9.0   **KNOWLEDGE OF SUPERVISION, MANAGEMENT, AND LAWS AND LEGISLATION THAT APPLY TO THE LEARNING ENVIRONMENT**

SKILL 9.1   **Identify procedures for selecting and maintaining appropriate equipment and facilities to enhance student learning.**

School officials and instructors should base **equipment selection** on the designated department budget, the benchmark and standard requirements (in Florida referred to as *Sunshine State Standards*) that the state requires to be included in the curriculum (for example, Team Sports is a required P.E. course for all high school student's in the State of Florida. Clearly P.E. teachers need to make sure they have the appropriate equipment for the required sports to be taught, such as volleyball and basketball), quality (how long will the equipment last) and, adaptability to varying and diverse abilities P.E. curriculums are laid out by each state and thus P.E. teachers must purchase equipment, within their district and school allotted budget, that will provide the materials necessary to meet these requirements.

Additional Guidelines for Selection of Equipment:

- Follow purchasing policies.

- Relate purchases to program, budget, and finances.

- Consider maintenance.

- Abide by legal regulations.

- Recognize administrative considerations (good working relationships at all personnel levels).

- Determine best value for money spent.

- Ensure that participants have their own equipment and supplies when this is necessary.

- Purchase from reputable manufacturers and distributors.

- Follow competitive purchasing regulations.

- Use school forms that have clearly identified brand, trademark, and catalog specifications.

- Stay within the budget allocated by the district and school.

Equipment Maintenance Procedures:

- Inspect supplies and equipment upon arrival.
- Label the supplies and equipment with organization's identification.
- Have policies for issuing and returning supplies and equipment.
- Keep equipment in perfect operating condition.
- Store equipment and supplies properly.
- Properly clean and care for equipment (including garments).

Facility Selection Considerations:

- Bond issues for construction.
- Availability of sites to girls, women, minorities, and the handicapped.
- Energy costs and conservation.
- Community involvement.
- Convertibility (movable walls/partitions).
- Environment must be safe, attractive, clean, comfortable, practical, and adaptable to individual needs.
- Compliance with public health codes.
- Effective disease control.

Facility Maintenance Procedures:

- Custodial staff, participants, and the physical education and athletic staffs must work together to properly maintain facility.
- Water temperature, hydrogen ion concentration, and chlorine levels of pools need daily monitoring (in Florida, however, public schools are no longer able or allowed to offer pool instruction or to have pools on their property due to liability issues arising from past lawsuits).
- Gymnasium play areas must be free from dust and dirt.
- Showers and drying areas need daily cleaning and disinfection and participants' clothing should meet health standards to prevent odor and bacterial growth.

TEACHER CERTIFICATION STUDY GUIDE

- Outdoor playing fields must be free of rocks and holes, and of any uneven surfaces.

- Disinfect and clean drinking fountains, sinks, urinals, and toilets daily.

- Air out and sanitize lockers frequently.

SKILL 9.2 Identify organizational strategies that enhance classroom management.

Proper organization of classroom procedures and information presentation is critical to classroom management and fostering a positive learning environment.

Instructors should establish and clearly communicate procedures and rules to maintain an orderly classroom. Organizational strategies that enhance classroom management include grouping of students, pre-planning of classroom activities, and rotation of students through various activities. (*See Skill 9.3*)

Organizational strategies that enhance information presentation include balancing instructional delivery methods, planning a variety of activities to appeal to students with different learning profiles, and planning a proper progression of information delivery to promote continual learning. Clustering, prioritizing, and categorizing are three common approaches to the organization of information.

SKILL 9.3 Identify supervisory and behavioral management techniques that enhance student learning.

Adequate supervision and behavioral management in the classroom is essential to student learning. Instructors must establish and communicate procedures, rules, and consequences of misbehavior to promote order in the classroom. Physical education instructors face unique behavioral management challenges because activities often take place in large environments throughout which participants are dispersed. Techniques to consider when planning supervision and behavioral management include grouping students to achieve maximum compatibility, removing misbehaving students from activities, and establishing an orderly system to handle class procedures (e.g., activity time, instruction time, rotations, and clean up). The P.E. teachers' code of classroom management is consistency, consistency, consistency in handling behavior problems.

KNOWLEDGE OF APPROPRIATE BEHAVIOR IN PHYSICAL EDUCATION ACTIVITIES

Appropriate Student Etiquette/Behaviors include: following the rules and accepting the consequences of unfair action, good sportsmanship, respecting the rights of other students, reporting own accidents and mishaps, not engaging in inappropriate behavior under peer pressure, encouragement, cooperation, paying attention to instructions and demonstrations, moving to assigned places and remaining in own space, complying with directions, practicing as instructed, properly using equipment, and not interfering with the practice of others.

Appropriate Content Etiquette/Behaviors include the teacher describing the performance of tasks and students engaging in the task, the teacher assisting students with task performance, and the teacher adjusting and developing tasks.

Appropriate Management Etiquette/Behaviors include the teacher directing the management of equipment, students, and space prior to practicing tasks; students getting equipment and partners; the teacher requesting that students refrain from "fooling around."

SKILL 9.4 Determine appropriate action for the care and prevention of injuries in physical education.

STRATEGIES FOR INJURY PREVENTION

Participant screening – evaluate injury history, anticipate and prevent potential injuries, watch for hidden injuries and for the reoccurrence of an injury, and maintain communication.

Standards and discipline – ensure that athletes obey rules of sportsmanship, supervision, and biomechanics.

Education and knowledge – stay current in knowledge of first aid, sports medicine, sport technique, and injury prevention through clinics, workshops, and communication with staff and trainers.

Conditioning – programs should be year long and participants should have access to conditioning facilities in and out of season to produce more fit and knowledgeable athletes who are less prone to injury.

Equipment – perform regular inspections and ensure proper fit and proper use.

Facilities – maintain standards and use safe equipment.

Field care – establish emergency procedures for serious injury.

Rehabilitation – use objective measures such as the power output on an isokinetic dynamometer.

Weather Conditions- use common sense and always err on the side of caution in extreme heat/cold or possible stormy weather; P.E. Instructors in Florida may be required to utilize a lightning detector when electrical storms are known to be moving towards or in the area. This allows instructors to monitor the number of cloud-to-ground lightning strikes in the surrounding area.

PREVENTION OF COMMON ATHLETIC INJURIES

Foot – start with good footwear, foot exercises.

Ankle – use high top shoes and tape support; strengthen plantar flexors (calf), dorsiflexiors (shin), and ankle eversion (ankle outward).

Shin splints – strengthen ankle dorsiflexors.

Achilles tendon – stretch dorsiflexion, strengthen plantar flexion (heel raises).

Knee – increase strength and flexibility of calf and thigh muscles.

Back – use proper body mechanics.

Tennis elbow – lateral epicondylitis caused by bent elbow, hitting late, not stepping into the ball, heavy rackets, and rackets that are strung too tight.

Head and neck injuries – avoid dangerous techniques (i.e. grabbing face mask) and carefully supervise potentially dangerous activities on the trampoline.

CARE OF COMMON ATHLETIC INJURIES

The most common injuries that physical education instructors will encounter include muscle sprains and strains, soft tissue injuries, and cuts and bruises. Instructors should apply the RICE principle when caring for muscle sprains, strains, and soft tissue injuries. The RICE principle stands for: rest, ice, compression, and elevation.

- **Rest** – injured students should stop using the injured body part immediately.

- **Ice** – the instructor should apply ice to the injured area immediately to help reduce swelling.

- **Compression** – the instructor should wrap the injured area to help reduce swelling.

- **Elevation** – the student should raise the injured area above the level of the heart.

In addition, physical education instructors should have a well-stocked first aid kit containing supplies to allow the treatment of routine cuts and bruises. Finally, instructors must recognize more serious injuries that require immediate medical attention. For example, injuries to the head or neck require medical attention and extreme caution.

SKILL 9.5 Identify major federal and state legislation that impacts physical education.

GRADUATION REQUIREMENTS

Education reforms enacted by the 1983 Florida legislature included for the first time in Florida's history statewide minimum high school graduation requirements.

Beginning with the 1986/87 school year, students must successfully complete a minimum of 24 credits in grades nine through twelve to graduate. The law specifies 15 of the 24 credits.

Included in the specified 15 credits are the following: one credit in physical education (**Personal Fitness and Team Sport are required classes**), one half-credit in performing and fine arts (selected from music, dance, drama, or art form that requires manual dexterity), and one-half credit in life management skills (to include consumer education, positive emotional development, nutrition, information and instruction on breast cancer detection and breast self-examination, cardiopulmonary resuscitation, drug education, and information regarding the health hazards of smoking).

The legislation encourages school to exceed established requirements for high school graduation. School districts vary in physical education requirements. Some require two credits, some one and a half, some one credit and some require the minimum one-half credit.

ESTABLISHMENT OF CURRICULUM FRAMEWORKS AND STUDENT PERFORMANCE STANDARDS

A curriculum framework is a set of broad guidelines that aids educational personnel in producing specific instructional plans for a given subject or study area. The legislative intent was to promote a degree of **uniformity and instructional consistency** in curriculum offerings.

Student achievement is related to the intended outcomes of the selected curriculum frameworks. The legislature developed student performance standards for 40 physical education courses and 15 dance courses.

FEDERAL LEGISLATION

The Department of Health and Human Services recommended legislative changes - including those for education. **Title IX** prohibits sex discrimination in educational programs and **PL 94-142** requires schools to provide educational services for handicapped students.

STATE LEGISLATION

State governments (Department of Education) are primarily responsible for education. Departments of education establish policies regarding course curricula, number of class days and class time, and the number of credits required for graduation.

IMPACT OF EDUCATION REFORMS

Enrollment increased and there was renewed administrative, parental, and student support.

Additional impact includes: coeducational classes, separate teams for boys and girls and men and women (otherwise the school must create a coeducational team), equal opportunities for both sexes (for facilities, equipment and supplies, practice and games, medical and training services, academic tutoring and coaching, travel and per diem allowances, and dining and housing facilities), and equitable expenditure of funds for both sexes.

Title IX takes precedence over all conflicting state and local laws and conference regulations. Federal aid (even aid not related to physical education or athletics) must comply with Title IX. Finally, Title IX prohibits discrimination in personnel standards and scholarships selection.

SKILL 9.6 Identify areas of legal liability applicable to physical education.

Historically, common-law rules stated that individuals could not sue government agencies without consent of the agencies. However, federal and state courts have begun to allow individuals to sue both federal and state governments. Thus, public schools and school districts are now subject to liability lawsuits.

Compulsory elements of the school curriculum, such as physical education, prompt courts to decide based on what is in the best interests of the public.

Although school districts still have immunity in many states, teachers do not have such immunity. Whether employed by private person or a municipal corporation, it is the duty of every employee not to injure another through the commission of negligent acts.

The following is a list of common legal terms and conditions applicable to physical education.

1. **Tort** – a legal wrong resulting in a direct or indirect injury; includes omissions and acts both intended and unintended to cause harm.

2. **Negligence** – failing to fulfill a legal duty according to common reasoning; includes instruction and facility maintenance; instructors must consider sex, size, and skill of participants when planning activities and grouping students.

3. **In Loco Parentis** – acting in the place of the parent in relation to a child.

4. **Sports Product Liability** – liability of the manufacturer to the person using the manufacturer's product who sustains injury/damage as a result of using the product.

5. **Violence and legal liability**– (intentional injury in sports contests) – harmful illegal contact upon one person by another (referred to as battery).

6. **Physical education classes held off campus and legal liability** – primary concern is providing due care, which is the responsibility of management and staff members of sponsoring organization; failing to observe "due care" can result in findings of negligence.

7. **Attractive Nuisance** – an object that results in physical injury that the responsible party should have foreseen.

ACTIONS THAT CAN AVOID LAWSUITS

1. Knowing the health status of each person in the program.

2. Considering the abilities and skill levels of all participants when planning new activities.

3. Grouping students to equalize competitive levels.

4. Using safe equipment and facilities.

5. Organizing and supervising classes.

6. Never leaving a class unsupervised.

7. Knowing first aid (Do not diagnose or prescribe).

8. Keeping accident records.

9. Giving instruction prior to potentially dangerous activities.

10. Making sure that injured students get medical attention and examination.

11. Getting exculpatory agreements (parental consent forms).

12. Having a planned, written disposition for students who suffer injuries or become ill.

13. Providing a detailed accident report if one occurs.

14. Joining your district's union. The National Education Association, which is the umbrella for all district unions, currently protects teachers from lawsuits by legal representation and two million dollars in liability coverage. The union fee in Florida for teachers varies from school district to school district, however it is usually in the range of $25 to $40 a month.

SKILL 9.7 Identify guidelines and actions that promote safety.

ACTIONS THAT PROMOTE SAFETY

1. Having an instructor who is properly trained and qualified.

2. Organizing the class by size, activity, and conditions of the class.

3. Inspecting buildings and other facilities regularly and immediately giving notice of any hazards.

4. Avoiding overcrowding.

5. Using adequate lighting.

6. Ensuring that students dress in appropriate clothing and shoes.

7. Presenting organized activities.

8. Inspecting all equipment regularly.

9. Adhering to building codes and fire regulations.

10. Using protective equipment.

11. Using spotters.

12. Eliminating hazards.

13. Teaching students correct ways of performing skills and activities.

14. Teaching students how to properly and safely use the equipment.

TEACHER CERTIFICATION STUDY GUIDE

COMPETENCY 10.0   **KNOWLEDGE OF APPROPRIATE RULES, STRATEGIES, AND TERMINOLOGY**

SKILL 10.1   **Apply appropriate rules and strategies of play to game and sport situations.**

APPLY APPROPRIATE RULES OF PLAY

ARCHERY:

- Arrows that bounce off or through the target count as 7 points.

- Arrows landing on lines between two rings receive the higher score of the two rings.

- Arrows hitting the petticoat receive no score.

BADMINTON:

- Intentionally balking opponent or making preliminary feints results in a fault (side in = loss of serve; side out = point awarded to side in).

- When a shuttlecock falls on a line it is in play (i.e. a fair play).

- If the striking team hits shuttlecock before it crosses net it is a fault.

- Touching the net when the shuttlecock is in play is a fault.

- The same player hitting the shuttlecock twice is a fault.

- The shuttlecock going through the net is a fault.

BASKETBALL:

- A player who touches the floor on or of the outside the boundary line is out-of-bounds.

- The ball is out-of-bounds if it touches anything (a player, the floor, an object, or any person) that is on or outside the boundary line.

- An offensive player remaining in the three-second zone of the free-throw lane for more than three seconds is a violation.

- A ball firmly held by two opposing players results in a jump ball.

- A throw-in is awarded to the opposing team of the last player touching a ball that goes out-of-bounds.

BOWLING:

- No score for a pin knocked down by a pinsetter (human or mechanical).

- There is no score for the pins when any part of the foot, hand, or arm extends or crosses over the foul line (even after ball leaves the hand) or if any part of the body contacts division boards, walls, or uprights that are beyond the foul line.

- There is no count for pins displaced or knocked down by a ball leaving the lane before it reaches the pins.

- There is no count when balls rebound from the rear cushion.

RACQUETBALL/HANDBALL:

- A server stepping outside the service area when serving faults.

- The server is out (relinquishes serve) if he/she steps outside of the serving zone twice in succession while serving.

- The server is out if he/she fails to hit the ball rebounding off the floor during the serve.

- The opponent must have a chance to take a position or the referee must call for play before the server can serve the ball.

- The ball is re-served if the receiver is not behind the short line when the ball is served.

- A served ball that hits the front line and does not land back of the short line is "short"; therefore, it is a fault. The ball is also short if it hits the front wall and two sidewalls before landing on the floor back of the short line.

- A serve is a fault when the ball touches the ceiling from rebounding off the front wall.

- A fault occurs when any part of the foot steps over the outer edges of the service or the short line while serving.

- A hinder (dead ball) is called when a returned ball hits an opponent on its way to the front wall - even if the ball continues to the front wall.

- A hinder is any intentional or unintentional interference of an opponent's opportunity to return the ball.

SOCCER:

The following are direct free-kick offenses:

- Hand or arm contact with the ball.

- Using hands to hold an opponent.

- Pushing an opponent.

- Striking/kicking/tripping or attempting to strike/kick/trip an opponent.

- Goalie using the ball to strike an opponent.

- Jumping at or charging an opponent.

- Kneeing an opponent.

- Any contact fouls.

The following are indirect free-kick offenses:

- Same player playing the ball twice at the kickoff, on a throw-in, on a goal kick, on a free kick, or on a corner kick.

- The goalie delaying the game by holding the ball or carrying the ball more than four steps.

- Failure to notify the referee of substitutions/re-substitutions and that player then handling the ball in the penalty area.

- Any non- player entering playing field without a referee's permission.

- Unsportsmanlike actions or words in reference to a referee's decision.

- Dangerously lowering the head or raising the foot too high to make a play.

- A player resuming play after being ordered off the field.

- An offensive player must have two defenders between him/her and the goal when a teammate passes the ball or else he is offsides.

- Attempting to kick the ball when the goalkeeper has possession or interference with the goalkeeper to hinder him/her from releasing the ball.

- Illegal charging.

TEACHER CERTIFICATION STUDY GUIDE

- Leaving the playing field without first obtaining the referee's permission while the ball is in play.

TENNIS:

A player loses a point when:

- The ball bounces twice on his/her side of the net.

- The player returns the ball to any place outside of designated areas.

- The player stops or touches the ball in the air before it lands out-of-bounds.

- The player intentionally strikes the ball twice with the racket.

- The ball strikes any part of a player or racket after making an initial attempt to hit the ball.

- A player reaches over the net to hit the ball.

- A player throws his racket at the ball.

- The ball strikes any permanent fixture that is out-of-bounds (other than striking the net).

    - a ball touching the net and landing inside the boundary lines is in play (except on the serve, where a ball contacting the net results in a "let" – replay of the point)

- A player fails, on two consecutive attempts, to serve the ball into the designated area (i.e. double fault).

VOLLEYBALL:

The following infractions by the receiving team result in a point awarded to the serving side and an infraction by serving team results in side-out:

- Illegal serves or serving out of turn.

- Illegal returns or catching or holding the ball.

- Dribbling or touching the ball twice in succession.

- Contact with the net (two opposing players making contact with the net at the same time results in a replay of the point).

- Touching the ball after it has been played three times without passing over the net.

- A player's foot completely touching the floor over the centerline.

- Reaching under the net and touching a player or the ball while the ball is in play.

- The players changing positions prior to the serve.

APPLY APPROPRIATE STRATEGIES

ARCHERY STRATEGIES FOR CORRECTING ERRORS IN AIMING AND RELEASING:

- Shifting position.

- Relaxing both the arms and shoulders at the moment of release.

- Reaching point of aim before releasing string.

- Pointing aim to the right or left of direct line between the archer and the target's center.

- Aiming with the left eye.

- Sighting with both eyes.

- Using the proper arrow.

BADMINTON STRATEGIES:

Strategies for Return of Service:

- Returning serves with shots that are straight ahead.

- Returning service so opponent must move out of his/her starting position.

- Returning long serves with an overhead clear or drop shot to near corner.

- Returning short serves with underhand clear or a net drop to near corner.

Strategies for Serving:

- Serving long to the backcourt near centerline.

- Serving short when opponent is standing too deep in his/her receiving court to return the serve, or using a short serve to eliminate a smash return if opponent has a powerful smash from the backcourt.

BASKETBALL STRATEGIES:

Use a Zone Defense:

- To prevent drive-ins for easy lay-up shots.

- When playing area is small.

- When team is in foul trouble.

- To keep a an excellent rebounder near the opponent's basket.

- When opponents' outside shooting is weak.

- When opponents have an advantage in height.

- When opponents have an exceptional offensive player, or when the best defenders cannot handle one-on-one defense.

Offensive Strategies Against Zone Defense:

- Using quick, sharp passing to penetrate zone forcing opposing player out of his/her assigned position.

- Overloading and mismatching.

Offensive Strategies for One-On-One Defense:

- Using the "pick-and-roll" and the "give-and-go" to screen defensive players to open up offensive players for shot attempts.

- Teams may use freelancing (spontaneous one-one-one offense), but more commonly they use "sets" of plays.

BOWLING FOR SPARES STRATEGIES:

- Identifying the key pin and determining where it must be hit to pick up remaining pins.

- Using the three basic alignments: center position for center pins, left position for left pins, and right position for right pins.

- Rolling the spare ball in the same way as for the first ball of the frame.

- Concentrating harder for the spare ball because of the reduced opportunity for pin action and margin of error.

HANDBALL OR RACQUETBALL STRATEGIES:

- Identifying the opponent's strengths and weaknesses.

- Making the opponent use less dominant hand or backhand shots if they are weaker.

- Frequently alternating fastballs and lobs to change the pace (changing the pace is particularly effective for serving).

- Maintaining position near the middle of court (the well) that is close enough to play low balls and corner shots.

- Placing shots that keep the opponent's position at a disadvantage to return cross-court and angle shots.

- Using high lob shots that go overhead but do not hit the back wall with enough force to rebound to drive an opponent out of position when he/she persistently plays close to the front wall.

SOCCER STRATEGIES:

- **Heading** – using the head to pass, to shoot, or to clear the ball.

- **Tackling** – the objective is to take possession of the ball from an opponent. Successful play requires knowledgeable utilization of space.

TENNIS STRATEGIES:

- Lobbing – using a high, lob shot for defense, giving the player more time to get back into position.

- Identifying an opponent's weaknesses and knowing one's own weaknesses to protect against them.

- Outrunning and out-thinking an opponent.

- Using change of pace, lobs, spins, approaching the net, and deception at the correct time.

- Hitting cross-court (from corner to corner of the court) for maximum safety and opportunity to regain position.

- Directing the ball where the opponent is not.

- Avoiding unforced errors and simply keeping the ball in play.

VOLLEYBALL STRATEGIES:

- Using forearm passes (bumps, digs, or passes) to play balls below the waist, to play balls that are driven hard, to pass the serve, and to contact balls distant from a player.

SKILL 10.2 Identify terminology for various physical education activities.

ARCHERY TERMINOLOGY:

- Addressing the target – standing ready to shoot with a proper stance.

- Anchor point – specific location on the archer's face to which index finger comes while holding and aiming.

- Archery golf (adaptation of golf to archery) – players shoot for holes, scoring according to the number of shots required to hit the target.

- Arm guard – a piece of leather or plastic worn on the inside of the forearm, protecting the arm from the bowstring.

- Arrow plate – a protective piece of hard material set into the bow where the arrow crosses it.

- Arrow rest – a small projection at the top of the bow handle where the arrow rests.

- Back – the side of the bow away from the shooter.

- Bow arm – the arm that holds the bow.

- Bow sight – a device attached to the bow through which the archer sights when aiming.

- Bow weight – designates the amount of effort needed to pull a bowstring a specific distance.

- Cant – shooting while holding the bow slightly turned or tilted.

- Cast – the distance a bow can shoot an arrow.

- Clout shooting – a type of shooting using a target 48 feet in diameter, laid on the ground at a distance of 180 yards for men, and 120 or 140 yards for women. Participants usually shoot 36 arrows per round.

- Cock/Index feather – the feather that is set at a right angle to the arrow nock; differently colored than the other two feathers.

- Creeping – letting the drawing hand move forward at the release.

- Crest – the archer's identifying marks located just below the fletchings.

- Draw – pulling the bow string back into the anchor position.

- End – a specific number of arrows shot at one time or from one position before retrieval of arrows.

- Face – the part of the bow facing the shooter.

- Finger tab – a leather flap worn on the drawing hand protecting the fingers and providing a smooth release of the bow string.

- Fletchings – the feathers of the arrow that give guidance to its flight.

- Flight shooting – shooting an arrow the farthest possible distance.

- Handle – the grip at the midsection of the bow.

- Hen feathers – the two feathers that are not set at right angles to the arrow nock.

- Instinctive shooting – aiming and shooting instinctively rather than using a bow sight or point-of-aim method.

- Limbs – upper and lower parts of the bow divided by the handle.

- Nock – the groove in the arrow's end where the string is placed.

- Nocking point – the point on the string where the arrow is placed.

- Notch – the grooves of the upper and lower tips of the limbs where the bow string is fitted.

- Over bow – using too strong a bow that is too powerful to pull a bowstring the proper distance.

- Overdraw – drawing the bow so the pile of the arrow is inside the bow.

- Petticoat – the part of the target face outside the white ring.

- Pile/point – the arrow's pointed, metal tip.

- Plucking – jerking the drawing hand laterally away from the face on the release causing the arrow's flight to veer to the left.

- Point-blank range – the distance from the target where the point of aim is right on the bull's eye.

- Point-of-aim – a method of aiming that aligns an arrow's pile with a target.

- Quiver – a receptacle for carrying or holding arrows.

- Recurve bow – a bow that is curved on the ends.

- Release – the act of letting the bowstring slip off the fingertips.

- Round – the term used to indicate shooting a specified number of arrows at a designated distance or distances.

- Roving – an outdoor archery game that uses natural targets (trees, bushes, stumps, etc.) for competition.

- Serving – the thread wrapped around the bowstring at the nocking point.

- Shaft – the long, body part of the arrow.

- Spine – the rigidity and flexibility characteristics of an arrow.

- Tackle – archery equipment referred to in its entirety.

- Target face – the painted front of a target.

- Trajectory – the flight path of the arrow.

- Vane – an arrow's plastic feather.

BADMINTON TERMINOLOGY:

- Alley – area on each side of a court used for doubles that is 1.5 feet wide.

- Around-the-head stroke – an overhead stroke used to hit a forehand-like overhead stroke that is on the backhand side of the body.

- Back alley – area between the baseline and the doubles long service line.

- Backcourt – the back third of the court.

- Backhand – a stroke made on the non-racket side of the body.

- Baseline – the back boundary line of the court.

- Bird – another name for the shuttlecock/shuttle.

- Block – a soft shot used mainly to defend a smash; intercepting opponent's smash and returning it back over the net.

- Carry/Throw – a call when the shuttle remains on the racket during a stroke. It is legal if the racket follows the intended line of flight.

- Centerline – the mid-line separating the service courts.

- Clear – a high shot that goes over the opponent's head and lands close to the baseline.

- Combination alignment – partners playing both up-and-back and side-by-side during doubles games and/or volleys.

- Crosscourt – a diagonal shot hit into the opposite court.

- Defense – the team or player hitting the shuttle upwards.

- Double hit – an illegal shot in which the player contacts the shuttle twice with the racket in one swing.

- Doubles service court – short, wide area to which the server must serve in doubles play.

- Down-the-line shot – a straight-ahead shot (usually down the sideline).

- Drive – a hard, driven shot traveling parallel to the floor (clears net but does not have enough height for opponent to smash).

- Drop – a shot just clearing the net and then falling close to it.

- Face – the racket's string area.

- Fault – an infraction of the rules resulting in loss of serve or a point awarded to the server.

- First serve – a term used in doubles play to indicate that the server is the "first server" during an inning.

- Foot fault – Illegal movement/position of the feet by the server or receiver.

- Forecourt – the front area of the court (between the net and the short service line).

- Forehand – a stroke made on the racket side of the body.

- Game point – the point, if won, that allows the server to win the game.

- Hand in – a term indicating that the server retains the serve.

- Hand out – a term that is used in doubles that denotes a player has lost the service.

- Home base – a center court position where a player can best play any shot hit by an opponent.

- Inning – the period a player or team holds service.

- Let – stopping the point because of some type of outside interference. The point is replayed.

- Lifting the shuttle – stroking the shuttle underhanded and hitting it upward.

- Long serve – a high, deep serve landing near the long service line in doubles or the back boundary line in singles.

- Love – the term used to indicate a zero score.

- Match – a series of games. Winning two of three games wins the match.

- Match point – the point, if won by the server, that makes that person the winner of the match.

- Midcourt – the middle-third of the court (between short service line and long service line for doubles).

- Net shot – a shot taken near the net.

- Non-racket side – the opposite side of the hand holding the racket.

- Offense – the team or player that is stroking the shuttle downward.

- Overhead – a motion used to strike the shuttle when it is above the head.

- Racket foot or leg – the foot or leg on the same side as the hand holding the racket.

- Ready position – the position a player assumes to be ready to move in any direction.

- Receiver – the player to whom the shuttle is served.

- Second serve – in doubles, the term indicates that one partner has lost the serve, and the other partner is now serving.

- Server – the player putting the shuttle into play.

- Setting – choosing the amount of additional points to play when certain tie scores are reached.

- Short-serve – a serve barely clearing the net and landing just beyond the short service line.

- Shuttlecock/Shuttle – the feathered, plastic or nylon object which is volleyed back and forth over the net.

- Side Alley – see alley.

- Smash – an overhead stroke hit downward with great velocity and angle.

- "T" – the intersection of the centerline and the short service line.

- Underhand – an upward stroke to hit the shuttle when it has fallen below shoulder level.

- Unsight – illegal position taken by the server's partner so the receiver cannot see the shuttle being hit.

- Up-and-back – an offensive alignment used in doubles. The "up" player is responsible for the forecourt and the "back" player is responsible for both.

BASKETBALL TERMINOLOGY:

- Backcourt players (Guards) – players who set up a team's offensive pattern and bring the ball up the court.

- Backdoor – an offensive maneuver in which a player cuts toward the baseline to the basket, behind the defenders, and receives a ball for a field goal attempt.

- Baseline – the end line of the court.

- Blocking/Boxing out – a term used when a player is positioned under the backboard to prevent an opposing player from achieving a good rebounding position.

- Charging – personal contact by a player with the ball against the body of a defensive opponent.

- Corner players (Forwards) – tall players that make up the sides of the offensive set-up who are responsible for the rebounding and shooting phases of the team's offense.

- Cut – a quick, offensive move by a player attempting to get free for a pass.

- Denial defense – aggressive individual defense to keep an offensive player from receiving a pass.

- Double foul – two opponents committing personal fouls against each other simultaneously.

- Dribble – ball movement by a player in control who throws or taps the ball in the air or onto the floor and then touches it. The dribble ends when the dribbler touches the ball with both hands concurrently, loses control, or permits it to come to rest while in contact with it.

- Drive – an aggressive move by a player with the ball toward the basket.

- Fake (Feint) – using a deceptive move with the ball pulling the defensive player out of position.

- Fast break – quickly moving the ball down court to score before the defense has a chance to set up.

- Field goal – a basket scored from the field.

- Freelance – no structure or set plays in the offense.

- Free-throw – the right given a player to score one or two points by unhindered shots for a goal from within the free throw circle and behind the free throw line.

- Give-and-go – a maneuver when an offensive player passes to a teammate and immediately cuts in toward the basket for a return pass.

- Held ball – occurs when two opponents have one or both hands firmly on the ball and neither can gain possession without undue roughness.

- Inside player (Center, Post, Pivot) – this player is usually the tallest team player who is situated near the basket, around the three-second lane area, and is responsible for rebounding and close-range shooting.

- Jump ball – a method of putting the ball into play by tossing it up between two opponents in the center circle to start a game or any overtime periods.

- Outlet pass – a term that designates a direct pass from a rebounder to a teammate (the main objective is starting a fast break).

- Overtime period – an additional period of playing time when the score is tied at the end of the regulation game.

- Personal foul – a player foul which involves contact with an opponent while the ball is alive or after the ball is in the possession of a player for a throw-in.

- Pick – a special type of screen where a player stands so the defensive player slides to make contact to free an offensive teammate for a shot or for a drive.

- Pivot – occurs when a player who is holding the ball steps once or more than once in any direction with the same foot while the other foot, called the pivot foot, remains at its point of contact with the floor. Also, another term for the inside player.

- Posting up – a player cutting to the three-second lane area, pausing, and anticipating a pass.

- Rebound – when the ball bounces off the backboard or basket.

- Restraining circles – three circles with a six-foot radius. One is located in the center of the court, and the others are located at each of the free-throw lines.

- Running time – not stopping the clock for fouls or violations.

- Screen – an offensive maneuver positioning a player between the defender and a teammate to free the teammate for an uncontested shot.

- Switching – defensive guards reversing their guarding assignments.

- Technical foul – a non-contact foul by a player, team, or coach for unsportsmanlike behavior or failing to abide by rules regarding submission of lineups, uniform numbering, and substitution procedures.

- Telegraphing a pass – a look or signal to indicate where the ball is going to be passed.

- Throw-in – a method of putting the ball in play from out-of-bounds.

- Traveling – illegal movement, in any direction, of a player in possession of the ball within bounds. Moving with the ball without dribbling.

- Violation – an infraction of rules resulting in a throw-in from out-of-bounds.

BOWLING TERMINOLOGY:

- Anchor – the teammate who shoots last.

- Baby split – the 1-7 or 3-10 pin railroads.

- Backup – a reverse hook rotating to the right for a right-handed bowler.

- Bed posts – the 7-10 railroad.

- Blow – an error or missing a spare that is not split.

- Box – a frame.

- Brooklyn – a crossover ball striking the 1-2 pocket.

- Bucket – the 2-4-5-8 or 3-5-6-9 leaves.

- Cherry – chopping off the front pin on a spare.

- Double – two consecutive strikes.

- Double pinochle – the 7-6 and 4-10 split.

- Crossover – same as a Brooklyn.

- Dutch 200 (Dutchman) – a score of 200 made by alternating strikes and spares for the entire game.

- Error – same as a "blow."

- Foul – touching or going beyond the foul line in delivering the ball.

- Frame – the box where scores are entered.

- Gutter ball – a ball that falls into either gutter.

- Handicap – awarding an individual or team a bonus score or score adjustment that is based on averages.

- Head pin – the number one pin.

- Hook – a ball that breaks to the left for a right-handed bowler and breaks to the right for a left-handed bowler.

- Jersey side – same as a Brooklyn.

- Kegler – synonym for a bowler.

- Lane – a bowling alley.

- Leave – pin or pins left standing after a throw.

- Light hit – hitting the head pin lightly to the right or left side.

- Line – a complete game as recorded on the score sheet.

- Mark – getting a strike or spare.

- Open frame – a frame in which no mark is made, leaving at least one pin standing after rolling both balls in a frame.

- Pocket – space between the head pin and pins on either side.

- Railroad – synonym for a split.

- Sleeper – a pin hidden from view.

- Spare – knocking all pins down with two balls.

- Split – a leave, after throwing the first ball, in which the number one pin plus a second pin are down, and when seven pins remain standing.

- Spot – a bowler's point of aim on the alley.

- Striking out – obtaining three strikes in the last frame.
- Tap – a pin that remains standing after an apparently perfect hit.
- Turkey – three consecutive strikes.

RACQUETBALL/HANDBALL TERMINOLOGY:

- Ace – a serve that completely eludes the receiver.
- Back-wall shot – a shot made from a rebound off the back wall.
- Box – see service box.
- Ceiling shot – a shot that first strikes the ceiling, then the front wall.
- Crotch – the junction of any two playing surfaces, as between the floor and any wall.
- Crotch shot – when a ball simultaneously strikes the front wall and floor (not good).
- Cut throat – a three-man game in which the server plays against the other two players. Each player keeps an individual score.
- Drive shot – a power shot against the front wall rebounding in a fast, low, and straight line.
- Fault – an illegally served ball.
- Handout – retiring the server who fails to serve legally or when the serving team fails to return a ball that is in play.
- Hinder – interference or obstruction of the flight of the ball during play.
- Kill – a ball rebounded off the front wall so close to the floor that it is impossible to return.
- Passing shot – a shot placed out of an opponent's reach on either side.
- Rally – continuous play of the ball by opponents.
- Receiving line – the broken line that is parallel to the short line on a racquetball court.
- Run-around shot – a ball striking one side wall, the rear wall, and the other side wall.

TEACHER CERTIFICATION STUDY GUIDE

- Safety zone – a five-foot area bounded by the back edge of the short line and receiving line that is only observed during the serve in racquetball.

- Screen – a hinder due to obstruction of the opponent's vision.

- Server – person in the "hand-in" position and eligible to serve.

- Service box – the service zone bounded by the side wall and a parallel line 18 inches away; denotes where server's partner must stand in doubles during the serve.

- Service court – the area where the ball must land when it is returned from the front wall on the serve.

- Service line – the line parallel to and five feet in front of the short line.

- Service zone – the area where the ball must be served.

- Short line – the line on the floor parallel to front wall and equidistant from the front and back wall. The serve must go over this line when returning from the front wall.

- Shoot – attempt kill shots.

- Side out – loss of serve.

- Thong – the strap on the bottom handle of the racquetball racquet that is worn around the player's wrist.

- Volley – returning the ball to the front wall before it bounces on the floor.

- Z-ball – defensive shot that strikes the front wall, a sidewall, and then the opposite side wall.

SOCCER TERMINOLOGY:

- Center – passing from the outside of the field near the side line into the center of the field.

- Charge – illegal or legal body contact between opponents.

- Chip – lofting the ball into the air using the instep kick technique; contacting the ball very low causing it to loft quickly with back spin.

- Clear – attempting to move the ball out of danger by playing the ball a great distance.

- Corner kick – a direct free kick from the corner arc awarded to the attacking player when the defending team last played the ball over their own end line.

- Cross – a pass from the outside of the field near the end line to a position in front of the goal.

- Dead ball situation – organized restarting of a game after stopping play.

- Direct free kick – a free kick whereby the kicker may score immediately from that initial contact.

- Dribble – the technique of a player self-propelling the ball with the foot in order to maintain control of the ball while moving from one spot to another.

- Drop ball – the method used to restart the game after temporary suspension of play when the ball is still in play.

- Goal area – the rectangular area in front of the goal where the ball is placed for a goal kick.

- Half-volley – contacting the ball just as it hits the ground after the ball has been airborne.

- Head – playing the ball with the head.

- Indirect free kick – a free kick from which a player, other than the kicker, must contact the ball before a goal can be scored.

- Kickoff – the free kick starting play at the beginning of the game, after each period, or after a score.

- Obstruction – illegally using the body to shield an opponent from reaching the ball.

- One-touch – immediately passing or shooting a received ball without stopping it.

- Penalty area – the large rectangular area in front of the goal where the goalkeeper is allowed to use the hands to play the ball.

- Penalty kick – a direct free kick awarded in the penalty area against the defending team for a Direct Free Kick foul.

- Settle – taking a ball out of the air and settling it on the ground so that it is rolling and no longer bouncing.

- Square pass – a pass directed toward the side of a player.

- Tackle – a technique to take the ball away from the opponents.

- Through pass – a pass penetrating between and past the defenders.

- Throw-in – the technique to restart the game when the ball goes out of play over the side line.

- Touchline – the side line of the field.

- Trap – the technique used to receive the ball and bring it under control.

- Two-touch- receiving – trapping and immediately re-passing the ball.

TENNIS TERMINOLOGY:

- Ace – serving a ball untouched by the opponent's racket.

- Advantage (Ad) – a scoring term. when the score is "deuce," the next point won.

- Alley – the 4.5-foot strip on either side of the singles court that is used to enlarge the court for doubles.

- Approach shot – a shot hit inside the baseline while approaching the net.

- Backcourt – the area between the service line and the baseline.

- Backhand – strokes hit on the left side of a right-handed player.

- Backspin – spin placed on a ball that causes the ball to bounce back toward the hitter.

- Back swing – the beginning of all ground strokes and service motion requiring a back swing to gather energy for the forward swing.

- Baseline – the end line of a tennis court.

- Break – winning a game in when the opponent serves.

- Center mark – a short mark bisecting the baseline.

- Center service line – the perpendicular line to the net dividing the two service courts in halves.

- Center strap – the strap at the center of the net anchored to the court to facilitate a constant 3-foot height for the net at its center.

- Center stripe – same as the center service line.

- Chip – a short chopping motion of the racket against the back and bottom side of the ball imparting backspin.

- Chop – placing backspin on a ball with a short, high-to-low forward swing.

- Cross-court – a shot hit diagonally from one corner of the court over the net into the opposite corner of the court.

- Cut off the angle – moving forward quickly against an opponent's cross-court shot, allowing the player to hit the ball near the center of the court rather than near the sidelines.

- Deep (depth) – a shot bouncing near the baseline on ground strokes and near the service line on serves.

- Default – a player who forfeits his/her position in a tournament by not playing a scheduled match.

- Deuce – a term used when the game score is 40-40.

- Dink – a ball hit very softly and relatively high to ensure its safe landing.

- Double fault – two consecutive, out-of-bounds serves on the same point resulting in loss of the point.

- Doubles lines – the outside sidelines on a court used only for doubles.

- Down-the-line – a shot hit near a sideline traveling close to, and parallel to, the same line from which the shot was initially hit.

- Drive – an offensive shot hit with extra force.

- Drop shot – a ground stroke hit so that it drops just over the net with little or no forward bounce.

- Drop volley – a volley hit in such a manner that it drops just over the net with little or no forward bounce.

- Error – a mistake made by a player during competition.

- Flat shot – a ball hit so no rotation or spin occurs when it is traveling through the air.

- Foot fault – illegal foot movement before service, penalized by losing that particular serve. Common foot faults are: stepping on or ahead of the baseline before the ball has been contacted and running along the baseline before serving.

- Forecourt – the area between the net and the service line.

- Forehand – the stroke hit on the right side of a right-handed player.

- Frame – the rim of the racket head plus the handle of the racket.

- Game – scoring term when a player wins 4 points before an opponent while holding a minimum 2-point lead.

- Grip – the portion of the racket that is grasped in the player's hand.

- Ground stroke – any ball hit after it has bounced.

- Half-volley – a ball hit inches away from the court's surface after the ball has bounced.

- Hold serve – winning your own serve. If you lose your own serve, your serve has been "broken."

- Let (ball) – a point replayed because of some kind of interference.

- Let serve – a serve that touches the net tape, falls into the proper square, and is played over.

- Linesman – a match official who calls balls "in" or "out."

- Lob – a ball hit with sufficient height to pass over the outstretched arm of a net player.

- Lob volley – a shot hit high into the air from a volleying position.

- Love – scoring term that means zero points or games.

- Match – a contest between two or four opponents.

- Match point – the point immediately before the final point of a match.

- Midcourt – area in front or in back of the service line of the playing court.

- Net ball – a ball that hits the net, falling on the same side as the hitter.

- No man's land – a general area within the baseline and proper net position area. When caught in that area, the player must volley or hit ground strokes near his/her feet.

- Offensive lob – a ball that is hit just above the racket reach of an opposing net player.

- Open face racket – a racket whose face is moving under the ball. A wide-open racket face is parallel to the court surface.

- Overhead – a shot hit from a position higher than the player's head.

- Over-hitting – hitting shots with too much force; over-hitting usually results in errors.

- Pace – the speed of the ball.

- Passing shot – a shot passing beyond the reach of the net player that lands inbounds.

- Poach – to cross over into your partner's territory in doubles in an attempt to intercept the ball.

- Racket face – the racket's hitting surface.

- Racket head – the top portion of the racket frame that includes the strings.

- Rally – opponents hitting balls back and forth across the net.

- Receiver – the player about to return the opponent's serve.

- Server – the player initiating play.

- Service line – the line at the end of the service courts parallel to the net.

- Set – a scoring term meaning the first player to win six games with a minimum two-game lead.

- Set point – the point, if won, which will give the player the set.

- Sidespin – a ball hit rotating on a horizontal plane.

- Signals in doubles – signaling your partner that you are going to poach at the net.

- Singles line – the sideline closest to the center mark that runs the entire length of the court.

- Slice – motion of the racket head going around the side of the ball, producing a horizontal spin on ball.

- Tape – the band of cloth or plastic running across the top of the net.

- Telegraphing the play – indicating the direction of one's intended target before hitting the ball.

- Topspin – forward rotation of the ball.

- Touch – the ability to make delicate, soft shots from several positions on the court.

- Twist – a special rotation applied to the ball during the serve causing the ball to jump to the left (of right-handed server).

- Umpire – the official that calls lines.

- Under spin – a counterclockwise spin placed on the ball (i.e. backspin).

- Volley – hitting the ball in the air before it bounces on the court.

VOLLEYBALL TERMINOLOGY:

- Attack – returning the ball across the net in an attempt to put the opponents at a disadvantage.

- Ball handling – executing any passing fundamental.

- Block – intercepting the ball just before or as it crosses the net.

- Bump – see forearm pass.

- Court coverage – a defensive player's court assignment.

- Dig – an emergency pass usually used to defend a hard-driven attack.

- Dink – a soft shot off the fingertips to lob the ball over a block.

- Double foul – infraction of rules by both teams during the same play.

- Drive – an attacking shot contacted in the center that attempts to hit the ball off the blocker's hands.

- Fault – any infraction of the rules.

- Forearm pass – a pass made off the forearms that is used to play served balls, hard-driven spikes, or any low ball.

- Free ball – a ball returned by the opponent that is easily handled.

- Front court – the playing area where it is legal to block or attack.

- Held ball – a ball that is simultaneously contacted above the net by opponents and momentarily held upon contact.

- Kill – an attack that cannot be returned.

- Lob – a soft attack contacted on the back bottom-quarter of the ball causing an upward trajectory.

- Overhand pass – a pass made by contacting the ball above the head with the fingers.

- Overlap – an illegal foot position when the ball is dead, with an adjacent player putting another out of position.

- Play over – replaying the rally because of a held ball or the official prematurely suspending play. The server re-serves with no point awarded.

- Point – a point is scored when the receiving team fails to legally return the ball to the opponents' court.

- Rotation – clockwise rotation of the players upon gaining the ball from their opponents.

- Serve – putting the ball in play over the net by striking it with the hand.

- Set – placing the ball near the net to facilitate attacking.

- Setter – the player assigned to set the ball.

- Side out – side is out when the serving team fails to win a point or plays the ball illegally.

- Spike – a ball hit with top spin and with a strong downward force into the opponents' court.

- Spiker – the player assigned to attack the ball.

- Spike-roll – an attack that first takes an upward trajectory using the spiking action (with or without jumping).

- Topspin (Overspin) – applying forward spin to the ball during the serve, spike, or spike roll.

COMPETENCY 11.0   KNOWLEDGE OF PROFESSIONAL DEVELOPMENT AND ADVOCACY STRATEGIES

SKILL 11.1   Identify physical education professional organizations and activities that promote professional development.

1. **Amateur Athletic Union (AAU)** – protects amateur sports from becoming corrupted; conducts pre-Olympic trials.

2. **American Alliance for Health, Physical Education, Recreation, and Dance (AAHPERD)** – works with legislatures concerning education and research, works with president's council on physical fitness and sport, and influences public opinion. Various associations make up the alliance.

3. **American College of Sports Medicine** – promotes scientific studies of sports and conducts research and post-graduate work.

4. **National Association for Sport and Physical Education (NASPE)** – a non-profit, professional membership organization that is the preeminent national authority on physical education; **developed national standards for physical education.**

5. **National Intramural Association**

6. **National Junior College Athletic Association**

7. **Phi Epsilon Kappa** – a fraternity for people pursuing careers in health, physical education, recreation, or safety.

SKILL 11.2   Identify current professional literature, research, and other sources of information that enhance professional growth.

1. AAU Publication Amateur Athlete Yearbook, AAU News (monthly)

2. American Academy of PE – position papers, studies for and by the academy.

3. Journal of PE, Recreation, and Dance

4. Research Quarterly

5. School Health Review

6. The Foil – is the official publication of Delta Psi Kappa; newsletter: The Psi Kappa Shield.

7. NEA - Today's Education

8. National Jr. College Athletic Association

9. Journal of PE – published bi-monthly.

10. YMCA Magazine – public affairs news.

SKILL 11.3 Identify ways to advocate the goals, objectives, and values of a comprehensive physical education program.

An effective strategy for promoting the physical education curriculum is to relate physical education to the purposes and goals of the entire educational process. By providing satisfying, successful, and enriching experiences that are properly taught, physical educators shape a physically, mentally, and socially fit society. Advocates should relate physical education to the total educational process through the cognitive, affective, and psychomotor domains.

The following is a list of talking points for physical education advocates. These points emphasize how physical education positively affects student development:

Benefits of physical education in the Cognitive Domain

- contributes to academic achievement
- promotes higher thought processes via motor activity
- contributes to knowledge of exercise, health and disease
- contributes to an understanding of the human body
- contributes to an understanding of the role of physical activity and sport in American culture
- contributes to the knowledgeable consumption of goods and services

Benefits of physical education in the Affective Domain

- contributes to self-actualization, self-esteem, and a healthy response to physical activity
- contributes to an appreciation of beauty
- contributes to directing one's life toward worthy goals
- emphasizes humanism
- affords individuals opportunities to enjoy rich social experiences through play
- promotes cooperative play with others

- teaches courtesy, fair play, and good sportsmanship
- contributes to humanitarianism

Benefits of physical education in the Psychomotor Domain

- develops movement skills for participation in sports and other physical activities
- develops skills to utilize leisure hours in mental and cultural pursuits
- develops skills necessary to the preservation of the natural environment

TEACHER CERTIFICATION STUDY GUIDE

COMPETENCY 12.0　　KNOWLEDGE OF TECHNOLOGY

SKILL 12.1　Identify current technological resources for accessing information on physical activity and health.

The best sources for identifying current technological resources for accessing information on physical activity and health are the Internet and local district technology workshops. District workshops are an extremely valuable resource in obtaining additional knowledge of how to use technology to obtain more information on each teacher's specific subject, including physical education.

Internet resources form an important part of current technology, which helps in accessing information on physical activity and health. There are Internet sources, which also enable educators, students, performers, parents, and athletes to stay aware of up-to-date information and programs about physical activity and health.

Numerous websites also exist that allow educators as well as performers to know about the developments in the physical education training systems. Use of technological resources also helps students to grasp more knowledge about physical activity and health-related issues.

Some organizations such as the NASPE also provide information on physical fitness and health. For example, NASPE invites school districts nationwide to post their school wellness policy on the NASPE Forum.

Research also shows there are different types of devices that athletes can use to monitor physical activity and health. Such devices include virtual bicycles, rowing machines, and treadmills. Such technology helps instructors and students plan and implement workouts and view workout results.

SKILL 12.2 Identify appropriate uses of technology in the instructional process.

Technology is the application of science to commercial, educational, health-related, military, or industrial objectives. Technology includes the use of computers, calculators, communication devices (telephone, videoconference devices), or other devices and methodologies to achieve those objectives.

Technology has become vital in the instructional process because all grades, lesson plans, semester grades, descriptions of test and test grades, absences, tardies, and behavior issues can be recorded and shared with the appropriate parties via computers.

Successful physical education instructors integrate technology into the instructional process. Technology is not simply a practice tool or device without purpose. The use of a particular technological device or product of technology should be appropriate to the lesson content.

Instructors can use technology in a variety of ways to help students and athletes improve or learn. Some ways in which instructors can use technology include:

1. **Actual use of technology** – the teacher and the students use the technology in a "hands-on" setting. For example, students use a video or digital camera in physical education to analyze their skills.

2. **Use of products of technology** – the use of products of technology in instruction and learning may include gathering information or resources from the Internet, imaging results for analyzing a motor skill, etc. In such a situation, the teacher can use the technology, or the products of technology, to present information, to provide examples and illustrations, and as a medium for providing instruction.

Some examples of technology-mediated instruction currently available include audio technologies such as radio, telephone, voice mail, and audiocassettes; video technologies such as television, teleconferencing, compressed video, and prerecorded videocassettes; and information technologies such as stand-alone workstations, CD ROM prepackaged multimedia, e-mail, chat rooms, bulletin boards, and the World Wide Web.

TEACHER CERTIFICATION STUDY GUIDE

ANNOTATED LIST OF RESOURCES FOR PHYSICAL EDUCATION

This list identifies some resources that may help candidates prepare to take the Physical Education examination. While not a substitute for coursework or other types of teacher preparation, these resources may enhance a candidate's knowledge of the content covered on the examination. The references listed are not intended to represent a comprehensive listing of all potential resources. Candidates are not expected to read all of the materials listed below, and passage of the examination will not require familiarity with these specific resources. When available, we have provided a brief summary for the reference cited. We have organized the resources alphabetically and by content domain in subtest order.

GROWTH, MOTOR DEVELOPMENT, AND MOTOR LEARNING

Colvin, A. Vonnie; Nancy J.; and Walker, Pamela. (2000). *Teaching the Nuts and Bolts of Physical Education: Building Basic Movement Skills.* Champaign, IL: Human Kinetics.

> Provides foundational content knowledge in locomotor and manipulative skills. Topics include rolling, throwing, catching, passing, dribbling, striking, kicking, and punting.

Fronske, H. (2001). *Teaching Cues for Sports Skills* (2nd edition). San Francisco, CA: Pearson/Cummings.

> Designed to provide verbal and alternate teaching cues and point out common errors in a variety of sports.

Graham, George. (1992). *Teaching Children Physical Education: Becoming a Master Teacher.* Champaign, IL: Human Kinetics.

> Includes the skills and techniques that successful teachers use to make their classes more interesting and developmentally appropriate. A reference for K-5 teachers, P.E. department chairs and administrators.

Lawson, H.A. (1984). *Invitation to Physical Education.* Champaign IL: Human Kinetics.

> Shows students and practitioners how to apply basic business management principles to a variety of health promotion programs.

Pangrazi, Robert. (2004). *Dynamic Physical Education for Elementary School Children* (14th edition). San Francisco, CA: Pearson/Cummings.

    Provides step-by-step techniques for teaching physical education while navigating through today's challenging educational terrain.

Powers, S.K., and Howley, E.T. (2003). *Exercise Physiology* (5th edition). New York, NY: McGraw Hill.

    Explains theory of exercise science and physical education with application and performance models to increase understanding of classroom learning.

Schmidt, R.A., and Lee, T.D. (1999). *Motor Control Learning: A Behavioral Emphasis* (3rd Edition). Champaign: IL: Human Kinetics.

    Addresses many factors that affect the quality of movement behaviors and the ease with which students can learn them.

Sherrill, C. (1998). *Adapted Physical Activity, Recreation and Sport: Cross-disciplinary and Lifespan* (5th edition). Dubuque, IA: WCB McGraw Hill.

    Emphasizes attitude change, inclusion, and psychosocial perspectives for understanding individual differences.

Siedentop, D. (1994). *Sport Education.* Champaign, IL: Human Kinetics.

    Shows how sport can help students learn fair play, leadership skills, and self-responsibility, in addition to becoming competent players. Also shows physical educators how to implement effective sport education programs to achieve these goals.

Summers, J.J. (1992). *Approaches to the Study of Motor Control and Learning.* Amsterdam: Elsevier Science.

    Provides analysis of research with particular emphasis on the methods and paradigms employed and the future direction of their work.

Thomas, Katherine, et al. (2003). *Physical Education Methods for Elementary Teachers.* Champaign, IL: Human Kinetics.

    Takes a research approach and offers a user-friendly technique to applicable teaching modalities for physical education for grades K-12.

Winnick, J.P. (2000). *Adapted Physical Education and Sport* (3rd edition). Champaign, IL: Human Kinetics.

>Provides a thorough introduction for students preparing to work with individuals with disabilities in a variety of settings.

THE SCIENCE OF HUMAN MOVEMENT

Birrell, S., and Cole, C.L. (1994). *Women, Sport, and Culture*. Champaign, IL: Human Kinetics.

>A collection of essays that examine the relationship between sport and gender.

Grantham, W.C.; Patton, R.W. Winick, M.L.; and York, T.D. (1998). *Health Fitness Management*. Champaign, IL: Human Kinetics.

>Brings conventional business management principles and operational guidelines to the unconventional business of health and fitness.

Hall, S. (2003). *Basic Biomechanics*. Boston, MA: McGraw-Hill.

Hamill, J., and Knutzen, K. (1995). *Biomechanical Basis of Human Movement*. Hagerstown, MD: Lippincott, Williams & Wilkins.

>Integrates aspects of functional anatomy, physics, calculus, and physiology into a comprehensive discussion of human movement.

Hopper, Chris; Fisher, Bruce; and Muniz, Kathy. (1997). *Health-Related Fitness: Grades 1-2, 3-4, 5-6*. Champaign, IL: Human Kinetics.

>These three books provide a wealth of health and fitness information and are an excellent resource for classroom teachers with limited backgrounds in physical education.

Lawson, H.A. (1984). *Invitation to Physical Education*. Champaign, IL: Human Kinetics.

>Shows students and practitioners how to apply basic business management principles to a variety of health promotion programs.

Sample Test

1. Which of the following countries did not greatly influence the early development of P.E. in the States: (Easy) (Skill 1.1)

   A. Germany

   B. England

   C. Norway

   D. Sweden

2. What was the first state in the U.S. to require P.E. in its public schools?(Average Rigor) (Skill 1.1)

   A. Florida

   B. Massachusetts

   C. New York

   D. California

3. President Eisenhower was alerted to the poor fitness levels of American youths. How was the poor physical conditioning of youths discovered in the Eisenhower Administration? (Average Rigor) (Skill 1.1)

   A. By WWII Selective Service Examination

   B. By organizations promoting physical fitness

   C. By the Federal Security Agency

   D. By the Kraus-Webber Tests

4. The Round Hill School (a private school) in Massachusetts was the first school to require P.E. in its curriculum. What year was this? (Average Rigor) (Skill 1.1)

   A. 1792

   B. 1823

   C. 1902

   D. 1806

5. The educational philosophy that believes experience is the best teacher is: (Easy) (Skill 1.2)

   A. Naturalism

   B. Pragmatism

   C. Idealism

   D. Existentialism

6. Idealism believes in: (Rigorous) (Skill 1.2)

   A. The laws of nature

   B. Experience is the key

   C. Practice, practice, practice

   D. The mind is developed through acquisition of knowledge

7. What must a P.E. teacher consider in planning their curriculum? (Easy) (Skill 2.2)

   A. Each student's schedule

   B. Planning only activities that he/she knows the students will enjoy

   C. The easiest to grade curriculum

   D. Available facilities and equipment

8. Which of the following is not a class-management technique? (Average Rigor) (Skill 2.2)

   A. Explaining procedures for roll call, excuses, and tardiness

   B. Explaining routines for changing and showering

   C. Explaining conditioning

   D. Promoting individual self-discipline

9. A teacher who modifies and develops tasks for a class is demonstrating knowledge of which appropriate behavior in physical education activities? (Rigorous)(Skill 2.2)

   A. Appropriate management behavior

   B. Appropriate student behavior

   C. Appropriate administration behavior

   D. Appropriate content behavior

10. All of the following are strategies to assist in teaching students of diverse populations except: (Rigorous) (Skill 3.1)

    A. Have the less skilled students sit out certain activities

    B. Station rotations

    C. Group students by skill level

    D. Peer to peer assisting

11. An instructor notices that class participation is much lower than expected. By making changes in equipment and rules, the instructor applied which of the following concepts to enhance participation? (Rigorous)(Skill 3.2)

    A. Homogeneous grouping

    B. Heterogeneous grouping

    C. Multi-activity designs

    D. Activity modification

12. Using tactile clues is a functional adaptation that can assist which type of students?(Rigorous)(Skill 3.5)

    A. Deaf students

    B. Blind students

    C. Asthmatic students

    D. Physically challenged students

13. To determine student's progress and the effectiveness of teaching, instructors must plan for: (Rigorous) (Skill3.6)

    A. Measurement and evaluation opportunities

    B. Adherence to exercise

    C. Different grading policies for different students

    D. Lesson plans that are only applicable to what is easiest to grade

14. The affective domain of physical education contributes to all of the following except: (Rigorous) (Skill 4.2)

    A. Knowledge of exercise, health, and disease

    B. Self-actualization

    C. An appreciation of beauty

    D. Good sportsmanship

15. An instructor used a similar movement from a skill learned in a different activity to teach a skill for a new activity. The technique used to facilitate cognitive learning was: (Rigorous)(Skill 4.2)

    A. Conceptual thinking

    B. Transfer of learning

    C. Longer instruction

    D. Appropriate language

16. A teacher rewards students for completing tasks. Which method is the teacher using to facilitate psychomotor learning? (Average Rigor)(Skill 4.2)

    A. Task/Reciprocal

    B. Command/Direct

    C. Contingency/Contract

    D. Physical/Reflex

17. Playing "Simon Says" and having students touch different body parts applies which movement concept? (Average Rigor)(Skill 5.1)

    A. Spatial Awareness

    B. Effort Awareness

    C. Body Awareness

    D. Motion Awareness

18. Which movement concept involves students making decisions about an object's positional changes in space? (Rigorous)(Skill 5.1)

    A. Spatial Awareness

    B. Effort Awareness

    C. Body Awareness

    D. Motion Awareness

19. Applying the mechanical principles of balance, time, and force describes which movement concept? (Average Rigor)(Skill 5.1)

    A. Spatial Awareness

    B. Effort Awareness

    C. Body Awareness

    D. Motion Awareness

20. Having students move on their hands and knees, move on lines, and/or hold shapes while moving develops which quality of movement? (Average Rigor)(Skill 5.1)

    A. Balance

    B. Time

    C. Force

    D. Inertia

21. Students that paddle balls against a wall or jump over objects with various heights are demonstrating which quality of movement? (Rigorous)(Skill 5.1)

    A. Balance

    B. Time

    C. Force

    D. Inertia

22. Having students move in a specific pattern while measuring how long they take to do so develops which quality of movement?(Average Rigor)(Skill 5.1)

    A. Balance

    B. Time

    C. Force

    D. Inertia

23. There are two sequential phases to the development of spatial awareness. What is the order of these phases? (Rigorous)(Skill 5.1)

    A. Locating more than one object in relation to each object; the location of objects in relation to one's own body in space.

    B. The location of objects in relation to one's own body in space; locating more than one object in relation to one's own body.

    C. Locating more than one object independent of one's body; the location of objects in relation to one's own body.

    D. The location of objects in relation to one's own body in space; locating more than one object in relation to each object and independent of one's own body.

24. Coordinated movements that project a person over an obstacle are known as: (Easy)(Skill 5.2)

    A. Jumping

    B. Vaulting

    C. Leaping

    D. Hopping

25. Using the same foot to take off from a surface and land is which locomotor skill? (Easy)(Skill 5.2)

    A. Jumping

    B. Vaulting

    C. Leaping

    D. Hopping

26. Which nonlocomotor skill entails movement around a joint where two body parts meet? (Easy)(Skill 5.2)

    A. Twisting

    B. Swaying

    C. Bending

    D. Stretching

27. A sharp change of direction from one's original line of movement is which nonlocomotor skill? (Easy)(Skill 5.2)

    A. Twisting

    B. Dodging

    C. Swaying

    D. Swinging

28. Which manipulative skill uses the hands to stop the momentum of an object? (Rigorous)(Skill 5.2)

    A. Trapping

    B. Catching

    C. Striking

    D. Rolling

29. Picking up coins, tying shoes, and petting animals develop this nonlocomotor skill.(Easy)(Skill 5.2)

    A. Bending

    B. Stretching

    C. Turning

    D. Twisting

30. To enhance skill and strategy performance for striking or throwing objects, for catching or collecting objects, and for carrying and propelling objects, students must first learn techniques for: (Rigorous)(SkilII 5.2)

    A. Offense

    B. Defense

    C. Controlling objects

    D. Continuous play of objects

31. Which of the following is not a type of tournament? (Average Rigor)(Skill 5.2)

    A. Spiderweb

    B. Pyramid

    C. Spiral

    D. Round Robin

32. Which of the following is not a type of meet? (Average Rigor)(Skill 5.2)

    A. Extramural

    B. Intramural

    C. Interscholastic

    D. Ladder

33. Equilibrium is maintained as long as: (Average Rigor)(Skill 5.5)

   A. Body segments are moved independently.

   B. The center of gravity is over the base of support

   C. Force is applied to the base of support.

   D. The center of gravity is lowered.

34. Which of the following does not enhance equilibrium? (Average Rigor) (Skill 5.5)

   A. Shifting the center of gravity away from the direction of movement.

   B. Increasing the base of support.

   C. Lowering the base of support.

   D. Increasing the base of support and lowering the center of support.

35. All of the following affect force Except(Easy)(Skill 5.5)

   A. Magnitude

   B. Energy

   C. Motion

   D. Mass

36. For a movement to occur, applied force must overcome inertia of an object and any other resisting forces. What concept of force does this describe? (Rigorous)(Skill 5.5)

   A. Potential energy

   B. Magnitude

   C. Kinetic energy

   D. Absorption

37. The energy of an object to do work while recoiling is which type of potential energy?(Average)(Skill 5.5)

   A. Absorption

   B. Kinetic

   C. Elastic

   D. Torque

38. Gradually decelerating a moving mass by utilization of smaller forces over a long period of time is: (Average)(Skill 5.5)

   A. Stability

   B. Equilibrium

   C. Angular force

   D. Force absorption

39. The tendency of a body/object to remain in its present state of motion unless some force acts to change it is which mechanical principle of motion? (Average Rigor) (Skill 5.5)

   A. Acceleration

   B. Inertia

   C. Action/Reaction

   D. Linear motion

40. The movement response of a system depends not only on the net external force, but also on the resistance to movement change. Which mechanical principle of motion does this definition describe? (Rigorous)(Skill 5.5)

   A. Acceleration

   B. Inertia

   C. Action/Reaction

   D. Air Resistance

41. Which of the following mechanical principles of motion states that every motion has a similar, contrasting response? (Easy)(Skill 5.5)

   A. Acceleration

   B. Inertia

   C. Action/Reaction

   D. Centripetal force

42. Which of the following principles is not a factor to assess to correct errors in performance for process assessment?(Average Rigor)(Skill 5.5)

   A. Inertia

   B. Action/Reaction

   C. Force

   D. Acceleration

43. A subjective, observational approach to identifying errors in the form, style, or mechanics of a skill is accomplished by:(Rigorous)(Skill 5.6)

   A. Product assessment

   B. Process assessment

   C. Standardized norm-referenced tests

   D. Criterion-referenced tests

44. What type of assessment objectively measures skill performance?(Rigorous)(Skill 5.6)

   A. Process assessment

   B. Product assessment

   C. Texas PE Test

   D. Iowa Brace Test

45. Process assessment does not identify which of the following errors in skill performance. (Average Rigor)(Skill 5.6)

   A. Style

   B. Form

   C. End result

   D. Mechanics

46. Determining poor performance of a skill using process assessment can best be accomplished by:(Average Rigor)(Skill 5.6)

   A. Observing how fast a skill is performed.

   B. Observing how many skills are performed.

   C. Observing how far or how high a skill is performed.

   D. Observing several attributes comprising the entire performance of a skill.

47. Which of the following methods measures fundamental skills using product assessment?(Rigorous)(Skill 5.6)

   A. Criterion-referenced tests

   B. Standardized norm-referenced tests

   C. Both A and B

   D. Neither A nor B

48. Product assessment measures all of the following except(Rigorous)(Skill 5.6)

   A. How the student performs the mechanics of a skill.

   B. How many times the student performs a skill.

   C. How fast the student performs a skill.

   D. How far or high the student performs a skill.

49. Instructors can evaluate skill level of achievement in archery by(Average Rigor)(Skill 5.6)

    A. Giving students a written exam on terminology.

    B. Having students demonstrate the correct tension of arrow feathers.

    C. Totaling a student's score obtained on the target's face.

    D. Time how long a student takes to shoot all arrows.

50. Instructors can determine skill level achievement in golf by(Average Rigor)(skill 5.6)

    A. The number of "birdies" that a student makes.

    B. The number of "bogies" a student makes.

    C. The score obtained after several rounds

    D. The total score achieved throughout the school year.

51. Instructors can determine skill level achievement in swimming by (Average Rigor)(Skill 5.6)

    A. How long a student can float

    B. How many strokes it takes a student to swim a specified distance.

    C. How long a student can stay under the water without moving.

    D. How many times a student can dive in five minutes.

52. Instructors can assess skill level achievement in bowling by: (Easy)(Skill 5.6)

    A. Calculating a student's average score.

    B. Calculating how many gutter-balls the student threw.

    C. Calculating how many strikes the student threw.

    D. Calculating how many spares the student threw.

53. What is the proper order of sequential development for the acquisition of locomotor skills?(Rigorous)(Skill 5.7)

   A. Creep, crawl, walk, jump, run, slide, gallop, hop, leap, skip; step-hop.

   B. Crawl, walk, creep, slide, walk, run, hop, leap, gallop, skip; step-hop.

   C. Creep, crawl, walk, slide, run, hop, leap, skip, gallop, jump; step-hop.

   D. Crawl, creep, walk, run, jump, hop, gallop, slide, leap, skip; step-hop.

54. Having students pretend they are playing basketball or trying to catch a bus develops which locomotor skill?(Easy)(Skill 5.7)

   A. Galloping

   B. Running

   C. Leaping

   D. Skipping

55. Having students play Fox and Hound develops: (Easy)(Skill 5.7)

   A. Galloping

   B. Hopping

   C. Stepping-hopping

   D. Skipping

56. Having students take off and land with both feet together develops which locomotor skill? (Easy)(Skill 5.7)

   A. Hopping

   B. Jumping

   C. Leaping

   D. Skipping

57. What is the proper sequential order of development for the acquisition of nonlocomotor skills?(Average Rigor)(Skill 5.7)

   A. Stretch, sit, bend, turn, swing, twist, shake, rock & sway, dodge; fall.

   B. Bend, stretch, turn, twist, swing, sit, rock & sway, shake, dodge; fall.

   C. Stretch, bend, sit, shake, turn, rock & sway, swing, twist, dodge; fall.

   D. Bend, stretch, sit, turn, twist, swing, sway, rock & sway, dodge; fall.

58. Activities such as pretending to pick fruit off a tree or reaching for a star develop which non-locomotor skill? (Easy)(Skill 5.7)

   A. Bending

   B. Stretching

   C. Turning

   D. Twisting

59. Having students collapse in their own space or lower themselves as though they are a raindrop or snowflake develops this nonlocomotor skill.(Easy)(Skill 5.7)

   A. Dodging

   B. Shaking

   C. Swinging

   D. Falling

60. Which is the proper sequential order of development for the acquisition of manipulative skills?(Rigorous)(Skill 5.7)

   A. Striking, throwing, bouncing, catching, trapping, kicking, ball rolling; volleying.

   B. Striking, throwing, kicking, ball rolling, volleying, bouncing, catching; trapping.

   C. Striking, throwing, catching, trapping, kicking, ball rolling, bouncing; volleying.

   D. Striking, throwing, kicking, ball rolling, bouncing; volleying.

61. Having students hit a large balloon with both hands develops this manipulative skill.(Average Rigor)(Skill 5.7)

   A. Bouncing

   B. Striking

   C. Volleying

   D. Trapping

62. Progressively decreasing the size of a target that balls are projected at develops which manipulative skill.(Average Rigor)(Skill 5.7)

   A. Throwing

   B. Trapping

   C. Volleying

   D. Kicking

63. Hitting a stationary object while in a fixed position, then incorporating movement, develops this manipulative skill.(Average Rigor)(Skill 5.7)

   A. Bouncing

   B. Trapping

   C. Throwing

   D. Striking

64. The ability for a muscle(s) to repeatedly contract over a period of time is: (Average Rigor)(Skill 6.1)

   A. Cardiovascular endurance

   B. Muscle endurance

   C. Muscle strength

   D. Muscle force

65. Students are performing trunk extensions. What component of fitness does this activity assess? (Average Rigor)(Skill 6.1)

   A. Balance

   B. Flexibility

   C. Body Composition

   D. Coordination

66. Data from a cardio-respiratory assessment can identify and predict all of the following except: (Rigorous)(Skill 6.1)

   A. Functional aerobic capacity

   B. Natural over-fatness

   C. Running ability

   D. Motivation

67. Data from assessing _____ identifies an individual's potential of developing musculoskeletal problems and an individual's potential of performing activities of daily living.(Rigorous0(Skill 6.1)

   A. Flexibility

   B. Muscle endurance

   C. Muscle strength

   D. Motor performance

68. The ability to rapidly change the direction of the body is: (Average Rigor)(Skill 6.2)

   A. Coordination

   B. Reaction time

   C. Speed

   D. Agility

69. Students are performing the vertical jump. What component of fitness does this activity assess? (Rigorous)(Skill 6.2)

   A. Muscle strength

   B. Balance

   C. Power

   D. Muscle endurance

70. Which of the following applies the concept of progression? (Rigorous)(Skill 6.3)

   A. Beginning a stretching program every day.

   B. Beginning a stretching program with 3 sets of reps.

   C. Beginning a stretching program with ballistic stretching.

   D. Beginning a stretching program holding stretches for 15 seconds and work up to holding stretches for 60 seconds.

71. Which of following overload principles does not apply to improving body composition? (Average Rigor)(Skill 6.3)

   A. Aerobic exercise three times per week.

   B. Aerobic exercise at a low intensity.

   C. Aerobic exercise for about an hour.

   D. Aerobic exercise in intervals of high intensity.

72. Which of the following principles of progression applies to improving muscle endurance? (Average Rigor)(Skill 6.3)

   A. Lifting weights every day.

   B. Lifting weights at 20% to 30% of assessed muscle strength.

   C. Lifting weights with low resistance and low reps.

   D. Lifting weights starting at 60% of assessed muscle strength.

73. The most important nutrient the body requires, without which life can only be sustained for a few days, is: (Easy)(Skill 6.4)

    A. Vitamins

    B. Minerals

    C. Water

    D. Carbohydrates

74. With regard to protein content, foods from animal sources are usually: (Average Rigor)(6.4)

    A. Complete

    B. Essential

    C. Nonessential

    D. Incidental

75. Fats with room for two or more hydrogen atoms per molecule-fatty acid chain are: (Rigorous)(Skill 6.4)

    A. Monounsaturated

    B. Polyunsaturated

    C. Hydrosaturated

    D. Saturated

76. An adequate diet to meet nutritional needs consists of: (Rigorous)(Skill 6.4)

    A. No more than 30% caloric intake from fats, no more than 50 % caloric intake from proteins, and at least 20% caloric intake from carbohydrates.

    B. No more than 30% caloric intake from fats, no more than 40% caloric intake from proteins, and at least 30% caloric intake from carbohydrates.

    C. No more than 30% caloric intake from fats, no more than 15% caloric intake from proteins, and at least 55% caloric intake from carbohydrates.

    D. No more than 30 % caloric intake from fats, no more than 30% caloric intake from proteins, and at least 40% caloric intake from carbohydrates

77. Maintaining body weight is best accomplished by: (Average Rigor)(Skill 6.4)

    A. Dieting

    B. Aerobic exercise

    C. Lifting weights

    D. Equalizing caloric intake relative to output

78. Most high-protein diets: (Average Rigor)(Skill 6.4)

   A. Are high in cholesterol

   B. Are high in saturated fats

   C. Require vitamin and mineral supplements

   D. All of the above

79. Which one of the following statements about low-calorie diets is false? (Rigorous)(Skill 6.4)

   A. Most people who "diet only" regain the weight they lose.

   B. They are the way most people try to lose weight.

   C. They make weight control easier.

   D. They lead to excess worry about weight, food, and eating.

80. Using the Karvonen Formula, compute the 60% - 80% THR for a 16-year old student with a RHR of 60. (Rigorous)(Skill 6.6)

   A. 122-163 beats per minute

   B. 130-168 beats per minute

   C. 142-170 beats per minute

   D. 146-175 beats per minute

81. Using Cooper's Formula, compute the THR for a 15 year old student.(Rigorous)(Skill 6.6)

   A. 120- 153 beats per minute

   B. 123-164 beats per minute

   C. 135-169 beats per minute

   D. 147-176 beats per minute

82. Aerobic dance develops or improves each of the following skills or health components except… (Rigorous)(Skill 6.6)

   A. Cardio-respiratory function

   B. Body composition

   C. Coordination

   D. Flexibility

83. Rowing develops which health or skill related component of fitness? (Rigorous)(Skill 6.6)

   A. Muscle endurance

   B. Flexibility

   C. Balance

   D. Reaction time

84. Calisthenics develops all of the following health and skill related components of fitness except: (Rigorous)(Skill 6.6)

    A. Muscle strength

    B. Body composition

    C. Power

    D. Agility

85. Which health or skill related components of fitness is developed by rope jumping? (Average Rigor) (Skill 6.6)

    A. Muscle Force

    B. Coordination

    C. Flexibility

    D. Muscle strength

86. Swimming does not improve which health or skill related component of fitness? (Rigorous)(Skill 6.6)

    A. Cardio-respiratory function

    B. Flexibility

    C. Muscle strength

    D. Foot Speed

87. A 17-year-old male student performed 20 sit-ups, ran a mile in 8 minutes, and has a body fat composition of 17%. Which is the best interpretation of his fitness level? (Rigorous)(Skill 6.6)

    A. Average muscular endurance, good cardiovascular endurance; appropriate body fat composition.

    B. Low muscular endurance, average cardiovascular endurance; high body fat composition.

    C. Low muscular endurance, average cardiovascular endurance; appropriate body fat composition.

    D. Low muscular endurance, low cardiovascular endurance; appropriate body fat composition.

88. Based on the information given in the previous question, what changes would you recommend to improve this person's level of fitness? (Average Rigor)(Skill 6.6)

    A. Muscle endurance training and cardiovascular endurance training.

    B. Muscle endurance training, cardiovascular endurance training, and reduction of caloric intake.

    C. Muscle strength training and cardio-vascular endurance training.

    D. No changes necessary.

89. Which of the following conditions is not associated with a lack of physical activity?
    (Average Rigor)(Skill 6.6)

    A. Atherosclerosis

    B. Longer life expectancy

    C. Osteoporosis

    D. Certain cancers

90. Which of the following pieces of exercise equipment best applies the physiological principles? (Average Rigor)(Skill 6.6)

    A. Rolling machine

    B. Electrical muscle stimulator

    C. Stationary Bicycle

    D. Motor-driven rowing machine

91. Working at a level that is above normal is which exercise training principle? (Rigorous)(Skill 6.7)

    A. Intensity

    B. Progression

    C. Specificity

    D. Overload

92. Students on a running program to improve cardio-respiratory fitness apply which exercise principle? (Rigorous)(Skill 6.7)

    A. Aerobic

    B. Progression

    C. Specificity

    D. Overload

93. Adding more reps to a weightlifting set applies which exercise principle? (Average Rigor)(Skill 6.7)

    A. Anaerobic

    B. Progression

    C. Overload

    D. Specificity

94. Which of the following does not modify overload? (Rigorous)(Skill 6.7)

    A. Frequency

    B. Perceived exertion

    C. Time

    D. Intensity

95. Prior to activity, students perform a 5-10 minute warm-up. Which is not recommended as part of the warm-up?(Easy)(Skill 6.7)

    A. Using the muscles that will be utilized in the following activity.

    B. Using a gradual aerobic warm-up.

    C. Using a gradual anaerobic warm-up.

    D. Stretching the major muscle groups to be used in the activity.

96. Which is not a benefit of warming up? (Rigorous)(Skill 6.7)

    A. Releasing hydrogen from myoglobin.

    B. Reducing the risk of musculoskeletal injuries.

    C. Raising the body's core temperature in preparation for activity.

    D. Stretching the major muscle groups to be used in the activity.

97. Which is not a benefit of cooling down? (Rigorous)(Skill 6.7)

   A. Preventing dizziness.

   B. Redistributing circulation.

   C. Removing lactic acid.

   D. Removing myoglobin.

98. Activities to specifically develop cardiovascular fitness must be: (Rigorous)(Skill 6.7)

   A. Performed without developing an oxygen debt

   B. Performed twice daily.

   C. Performed every day.

   D. Performed for a minimum of 10 minutes.

99. Overloading for muscle strength includes all of the following except: (Rigorous)(Skill 6.7)

   A. Raising heart rate to an intense level.

   B. Lifting weights every other day.

   C. Lifting with high resistance and low reps.

   D. Lifting 60% to 90% of assessed muscle strength

100. Physical Education is a key component of an interdisciplinary learning approach because : (Easy)(Skill 6.10)

   A. It is usually held outside

   B. It does not involve other subject areas

   C. It allows for students to burn off energy

   D. It draws from many other curriculum areas

101. Physiological benefits of exercise include all of the following except: (Average Rigor)(Skill 6.10)

   A. Reducing mental tension

   B. Improving muscle strength

   C. Cardiac hypertrophy

   D. Quicker recovery rate

102. Psychological benefits of exercise include all of the following except: (Rigorous)(Skill 6.10)

   A. Improved sleeping patterns

   B. Improved energy regulation

   C. Improved appearance

   D. Improved quality of life

103. Social skills and values developed by activity include all of the following except: Rigorous) (Skill 7.2)

    A. Winning at all costs

    B. Making judgments in groups

    C. Communicating and cooperating

    D. Respecting rules and property

104. All of the following are methods to evaluate the affective domain except: (Average Rigor)(Skill 8.2)

    A. Adams Prosocial Inventory

    B. Crowell Personal Distance Scale

    C. Blanchard Behavior Rating Scale

    D. McCloy's Prosocial Behavior Scale

105. Educators can evaluate the cognitive domain by all of the following methods except (Rigorous)(Skill 8.2)

    A. Norm-Referenced Tests

    B. Criterion Referenced Tests

    C. Standardized Tests

    D. Willis Sports Inventory Tests

106. Which is not a common negative stressor?(Rigorous))Skill 6.2)

    A. Loss of significant other

    B. Personal illness or injury.

    C. Moving to a new state.

    D. Landing a new job.

107. Which of the following is not a skill assessment test to evaluate student performance? (Average Rigor)(Skill 8.3)

    A. Harrocks Volley

    B. Rodgers Strength Test

    C. Iowa Brace Test

    D. AAHPERD Youth Fitness Test

108. All of the following are Systematic Observational Evaluations except: (Rigorous)(Skill 8.4)

    A. Reflective Recording

    B. Event Recording

    C. Duration Recording

    D. Self Recording

109. A physical education instructor anticipates and prevents potential injuries, watches for hidden injuries, and takes an injury evaluation of the entire class. Which of the following strategies to prevent injuries is the teacher demonstrating? (Average Rigor) (Skill 9.4)

   A. Maintaining hiring standards

   B. Proper use of equipment

   C. Proper procedures for emergencies

   D. Participant screening

110. In regard to injury prevention, RICE stands for: (Easy) (Skill 9.4)

   A. Raise, Ice, Compression, Elevation

   B. Rest, Ice, Compression, Elevation

   C. Rest, Inside, Compression, Elevation

   D. Raise, Inside, Compact, Elevation

111. Which of the following is not a state standard for P.E. in Florida ? (Rigorous) (Skill 9.5)

   A. Students are required to dress out for P.E. in all grades and all public schools

   B. Students are to understand the benefits of physical fitness

   C. Students are to learn certain motor skills to the best of their abilities

   D. Students are to be exposed to a variety of physical activities

112. Although Mary is a paraplegic, she wants to participate in some capacity in the physical education class. What federal legislative act entitles her to do so? (Rigorous)(Skill 9.5)

   A. PE 94-142

   B. Title IX

   C. PL 94-142

   D. Title XI

113. A legal wrong resulting in a direct or an indirect injury is: (Average Rigor)(Skill 9.6)

   A. Negligence

   B. A Tort

   C. In loco parentis

   D. Legal liability

114. All of the following actions help avoid lawsuits except: (Average Rigor) (Skill 9.6)

   A. Ensuring equipment and facilities are safe

   B. Getting exculpatory agreements

   C. Knowing each students' health status

   D. Grouping students with unequal competitive levels

115. Which of the following actions does not promote safety? (Rigorous) (Skill 9.6)

   A. Allowing students to wear the current style of shoes

   B. Presenting organized activities

   C. Inspecting equipment and facilities

   D. Instructing skill and activities properly

116. Although they are still hitting the target, the score of some students practicing archery has decreased as the distance between them and the target has increased. Which of the following adjustments will improve their scores? (Rigorous)(Skill 10.1)

   A. Increasing the velocity of their arrows.

   B. Increasing the students' base of support.

   C. Increasing the weight of the arrows.

   D. Increasing the parabolic path of the arrows.

117. Some students practicing basketball are having difficulty with "free throws," even though the shots make it to and over the hoop. What adjustment will improve their "free throws?"(Average Rigor)(Skill 10.1)

   A. Increasing the height of release (i.e. jump shot).

   B. Increasing the vertical path of the ball.

   C. Increasing the velocity of the release.

   D. Increasing the base of support.

118. An archery student's arrow bounced off the red part of the target face. What is the correct ruling?(Average Rigor)(Skill 10.1)

   A. No score.

   B. Re-shoot arrow.

   C. 7 points awarded.

   D. Shot receives same score as highest arrow shot that did not bounce off the target.

119. A student playing badminton believed that the shuttlecock was going to land out-of-bounds. The shuttlecock landed on the line. What is the correct ruling?(Easy)(Skill 10.1)

   A. The shuttlecock is out-of-bounds.

   B. The shuttlecock is in-bounds.

   C. The point is replayed.

   D. That player is charged with a feint.

120. A mechanical pinsetter accidentally knocked down the only bowling pin left standing for a spare attempt after clearing all the other pins knocked down by the first ball thrown. What is the correct ruling? (Rigorous)(Skill 10.1)

   A. Foul

   B. Spare

   C. Frame is replayed

   D. No count for that

121. The ball served in racquetball hits the front line and lands in front of the short line. What is the ruling?(Easy)(Skill 10.1)

   A. Fault

   B. Reserve

   C. Out-of-bounds

   D. Fair ball

122. Two opposing soccer players are trying to gain control of the ball when one player "knees" the other. What is the ruling?(Easy)(Skill 10.1)

   A. Direct free kick

   B. Indirect free kick

   C. Fair play

   D. Ejection from a game

123. Two students are playing badminton. When receiving the shuttlecock, one student consistently stands too deep in the receiving court. What strategy should the server use to serve the shuttlecock?(Average Rigor)(Skill 10.2)

   A. Smash serve

   B. Clear serve

   C. Overhead serve

   D. Short serve

124. A basketball team has an outstanding rebounder. In order to keep this player near the opponent's basket, which strategy should the coach implement?(Easy)(Skill 10.2)

   A. Pick-and-Roll

   B. Give-and-Go

   C. Zone defense

   D. Free-lancing

125. When a defensive tennis player needs more time to return to his position, what strategy should he apply?(Rigorous)(Skill 10.2)

   A. Drop shot

   B. Dink shot

   C. Lob shot

   D. Down-the-line shot

126. An overhead badminton stroke used to hit a forehand-like overhead stroke that is on the backhand side of the body is called Rigorous)(Skill 10.2)

   A. Around-the-head-shot

   B. Down-the-line shot

   C. Lifting the shuttle

   D. Under hand shuttle

127. A maneuver when an offensive player passes to a teammate and then immediately cuts in toward the basket for a return pass is: (Average Rigor)(Skill 10.2)

   A. Charging

   B. Pick

   C. Give-and-go

   D. Switching

128. A bowling pin that remains standing after an apparently perfect hit is called a: (Rigorous)(Skill 10.2)

   A. Tap

   B. Turkey

   C. Blow

   D. Leave

129. A soccer pass from the outside of the field near the end line to a position in front of the goal is called: (Average Rigor)(Skill 10.2)

   A. Chip

   B. Settle

   C. Through

   D. Cross

130. A volleyball that is simultaneously contacted above the net by opponents and momentarily held upon contact is called a/an: (Easy)(Skill 10.2)

   A. Double fault

   B. Play over

   C. Overlap

   D. Held ball

131. Volleyball player LB on team A digs a spiked ball. The ball deflects off of LB's shoulder. What is the ruling? (Average Rigor)(Skill 10.2)

   A. Fault

   B. Legal hit

   C. Double foul

   D. Play over

132. In 1956, the AAHPER Fitness Conferences established: (Rigorous) (Skill 11.1)

   A. The President's Council on Youth Fitness

   B. The President's Citizens' Advisory Committee

   C. The President's Council on Physical Fitness

   D. A and B

133. Which professional organization protects amateur sports from corruption? (Easy) (Skill 11.1)

   A. AIWA

   B. AAHPERD

   C. NCAA

   D. AAU

134. Which professional organization works with legislatures? Average Rigor) (Skill 11.1)

   A. AIWA

   B. AAHPERD

   C. ACSM

   D. AAU

135. Research in physical education is published in all of the following periodicals except the: (Average Rigor) (Skill 11.2)

   A. School PE Update

   B. Research Quarterly

   C. Journal of Physical Education

   D. YMCA Magazine

Rigor Table

Easy %20	Average Rigor %40	Rigorous %40
1, 5, 7, 24, 25, 26, 27, 29, 35, 41, 52, 54, 55, 56, 58, 59, 73, 95, 100, 110, 119, 121, 122, 124, 130, 133	2, 3, 4, 8, 16, 17, 19, 20, 22, 31, 32, 33, 34, 37, 38, 39, 42, 45, 46, 49, 50, 51, 57, 61, 62, 63, 64, 65, 68, 71, 72, 74, 77, 78, 84, 85, 88, 89, 90, 93, 101, 104, 107, 109, 113, 114, 117, 118, 123, 127, 129, 131, 134, 135	6, 9, 10, 11, 12, 13, 14, 15, 18, 21, 23, 28, 30, 36, 40, 43, 44, 47, 48, 53, 60, 66, 67, 69, 70, 75, 76, 79, 80, 81, 82, 83, 86, 87, 91, 92, 94, 96, 97, 98, 99, 102, 103, 105, 106, 108, 111, 112, 115, 116, 120, 125, 126, 128, 132

Answer Key

1.	C	36.	B	71.	A	106.	D
2.	D	37.	C	72.	B	107.	A
3.	D	38.	D	73.	C	108.	A
4.	B	39.	B	74.	A	109.	D
5.	B	40.	A	75.	B	110.	B
6.	D	41.	C	76.	C	111.	A
7.	D	42.	C	77.	D	112.	C
8.	C	43.	B	78.	D	113.	B
9.	D	44.	B	79.	C	114.	D
10.	A	45.	C	80.	D	115.	A
11.	D	46.	D	81.	B	116.	D
12.	B	47.	C	82.	D	117.	B
13.	A	48.	A	83.	A	118.	C
14.	A	49.	C	84.	C	119.	B
15.	B	50.	C	85.	B	120.	D
16.	C	51.	B	86.	D	121.	A
17.	C	52.	A	87.	C	122.	A
18.	A	53.	D	88.	A	123.	D
19.	A	54.	B	89.	B	124.	C
20.	A	55.	A	90.	C	125.	C
21.	C	56.	B	91.	D	126.	A
22.	B	57.	C	92.	C	127.	C
23.	D	58.	B	93.	B	128.	A
24.	B	59.	D	94.	B	129.	D
25.	D	60.	B	95.	C	130.	D
26.	C	61.	C	96.	A	131.	B
27.	B	62.	A	97.	D	132.	D
28.	B	63.	D	98.	A	133.	D
29.	A	64.	B	99.	A	134.	B
30.	C	65.	B	100.	C	135.	A
31.	C	66.	B	101.	A		
32.	B	67.	A	102.	B		
33.	B	68.	D	103.	A		
34.	A	69.	C	104.	D		
35.	D	70.	D	105.	D		

Rationales with Sample Questions

1. **Which of the following countries did not greatly influence the early development of P.E. in the States :   (Easy)(Skill 1.1)**

    A. Germany

    B. England

    C. Norway

    D. Sweden

(C.) Germany, England and Sweden were the three countries that most greatly influenced the influx and curriculum of physical education into the U.S.

2. **What was the first state in the U.S. to require P.E. in its public schools?(Average Rigor)(Skill 1.10)**

    A. Florida

    B. Massachusetts

    C. New York

    D. California

(D.) California in 1866.

3. **President Eisenhower was alerted to the poor fitness levels of American youths. How was the poor physical conditioning of youths discovered in the Eisenhower Administration? (Average Rigor) (Skill 1.1)**

   A. By WWII Selective Service Examination

   B. By organizations promoting physical fitness

   C. By the Federal Security Agency

   D. By the Kraus-Webber Tests

(D.) This is one of the programs that President Dwight Eisenhower implemented during his presidency. Using a test devised by Drs. Hans Kraus and Sonja Weber of New York Presbyterian Hospital, Bonnie began testing children in Europe, Central America, and the United States. The Kraus-Weber test involved six simple movements and took 90 seconds to administer. It compared US children to European children in the realms of strength and flexibility. The fitness emphasis in schools started by Kraus-Weber declined in the 1970s and early 1980s. The President's Council on Physical Fitness and Sports was one result of the Kraus-Weber test results.

4. **The Round Hill School (a private school) in Massachusetts was the first school to require P.E. in its curriculum. What year was this? (Average Rigor) (Skill 1.1)**

   A. 1792

   B. 1823

   C. 1902

   D. 1806

(B) The Round Hill School was the first school to require P.E. in its curriculum in 1823.

5. The physical education philosophy that is based on experience is: (Easy) (Skill 1.2)

    A. Naturalism

    B. Pragmatism

    C. Idealism

    D. Existentialism

(B.) Pragmatism, as a school of philosophy, is a collection of different ways of thinking. Given the diversity of thinkers and the variety of schools of thought that have adopted this term over the years, the term pragmatism has become almost meaningless in the absence of further qualification. Most of the thinkers who describe themselves as pragmatists indicate some connection with practical consequences or real effects as vital components of both meaning and truth.

6. Idealism believes in: (Rigorous) (Skill 1.2)

    A. The laws of nature

    B. Experience is the key

    C. Practice, practice, practice

    D. The mind is developed through acquisition of knowledge

(D.) Idealism believes in the "power of knowledge." The more the students know, the sharper the mind and body become.

7. . What must a P.E. teacher consider in planning their curriculum? (Easy) (Skill 2.2)

    A. Each student's schedule

    B. Planning only activities that he/she knows the students will enjoy

    C. The easiest to grade curriculum

    D. Available facilities and equipment

(D.) Without the facilities and equipment for an activity, clearly the activity cannot be held.

8. **Which of the following is not a class-management technique?(Average Rigor) (Skill 2.2)**

   A. Explaining procedures for roll call, excuses, and tardiness

   B. Explaining routines for changing and showering

   C. Explaining conditioning

   D. Promoting individual self-discipline

(C.) Explaining conditioning is not a class management technique. It is an instructional lesson.

9. **A teacher who modifies and develops tasks for a class is demonstrating knowledge of which appropriate behavior in physical education activities? (Rigorous) (Skill 2.2)**

   A. Appropriate management behavior

   B. Appropriate student behavior

   C. Appropriate administration behavior

   D. Appropriate content behavior

(D.) In this case, the teacher is demonstrating knowledge of a behavior in reference to physical activity. It is known as appropriate content behavior. The other options are not related to physical activities.

10. **All of the following are strategies to assist in teaching students of diverse populations except: (Rigorous) (Skill 3.1)**

    A. Have the less skilled students sit out certain activites

    B. Station rotations

    C. Group students by skill level

    D. Peer to peer assisting

(A.) Make sure all student's are participating at all times. Never sit out the less skilled students at anytime.

11. An instructor notices that class participation is much lower than expected. By making changes in equipment and rules, the instructor applied which of the following concepts to enhance participation? (Rigorous) (Skill 3.2)

   A. Homogeneous grouping

   B. Heterogeneous grouping

   C. Multi-activity designs

   D. Activity modification

(D.) The following is an example of activity modification. Wrist position is key to controlling carpal tunnel syndrome symptoms. The carpal tunnel is most narrow when the wrist is either bent down or cocked back all of the way. It is largest when the wrist is straight. For this reason, changing how you do repetitive hand activities or avoiding those activities altogether can help. For example, the more your wrist is bent, the more pressure is put on your median nerve.

12. Using tactile clues is a functional adaptation that can assist which type of students? (Rigorous) (Skill 3.5)

   A. Deaf students

   B. Blind students

   C. Asthmatic students

   D. Physically challenged students

(B.) Blind people use tactile clues to identify colors. Instructors should use tactile clues to help students see or hear targets by adding color, making them larger, or moving them closer. It will help cooperation in a creative way.

13. **To determine student's progress and the effectiveness of teaching, instructors must plan for: (Rigorous) (Skill 3.6)**

    A. Measurement and evaluation opportunities

    B. Adherence to exercise

    C. Different grading policies for different students

    D. Lesson plans that are only applicable to what is easiest to grade.

(A.) Student progress must always be measurable and able to be evaluated

14. **The affective domain of physical education contributes to all of the following except: (Rigorous) (Skill 4.2)**

    A. Knowledge of exercise, health, and disease

    B. Self-actualization

    C. An appreciation of beauty

    D. Good sportsmanship

(A.) The affective domain encompasses emotions, thoughts, and feelings related to physical education. Knowledge of exercise, health, and disease is part of the cognitive domain.

15. **An instructor used a similar movement from a skill learned in a different activity to teach a skill for a new activity. The technique used to facilitate cognitive learning was: (Rigorous) (Skill 4.2)**

    A. Conceptual thinking

    B. Transfer of learning

    C. Longer instruction

    D. Appropriate language

(B.) Using a previously used movement to facilitate a new task is a transfer of learning. The individual relates the past activity to the new one, enabling him/her to learn it more easily. Conceptual thinking is related to the transfer of learning, but it does not give the exact idea. Rather, it emphasizes the history of all learning.

16. A teacher rewards students for completing tasks. Which method is the teacher using to facilitate psychomotor learning? (Average Rigor) (Skill 4.2)

   A. Task/Reciprocal

   B. Command/Direct

   C. Contingency/Contract

   D. Physical/Reflex

(C.) Since the teacher is rewarding the student, the contingency/contract method is in place. The command/direct method involves the interaction between student and teacher when the student fails to fulfill the requirements.

17. Playing "Simon Says" and having students touch different body parts applies which movement concept? (Average Rigor) (Skill 5.1)

   A. Spatial Awareness

   B. Effort Awareness

   C. Body Awareness

   D. Motion Awareness

(C.) Body Awareness is a method that integrates European traditions of movement and biomedical knowledge with the East Asian traditions of movement (e.g. Tai chi and Zen meditation).

18. Which movement concept involves students making decisions about an object's positional changes in space? (Rigorous) (Skill 5.1)

   A. Spatial Awareness

   B. Effort Awareness

   C. Body Awareness

   D. Motion Awareness

(A.) Spatial awareness is the movement concept that involves students making decisions about an object's positional changes in space.

19. Applying the mechanical principles of balance, time, and force describes which movement concept? (Average Rigor) (Skill 5.1)

    A. Spatial Awareness

    B. Effort Awareness

    C. Body Awareness

    D. Motion Awareness

(A.) Spatial awareness is an organized awareness of objects in the space around us. It is also an awareness of our body's position in space. Without this awareness, we would not be able to pick food up from our plates and put it in our mouths. We would have trouble reading, because we could not see the letters in their correct relation to each other and to the page. Athletes would not have the precise awareness of the position of other players on the field and the movement of the ball, which is necessary to play sports effectively.

20. Having students move on their hands and knees, move on lines, and/or hold shapes while moving develops which quality of movement? (Average Rigor) (Skill 5.1)

    A. Balance

    B. Time

    C. Force

    D. Inertia

(A.) Balance is one of the physiological senses. It allows humans and animals to walk without falling. Some animals are better at this than humans. For example, a cat (as a quadruped using its inner ear and tail) can walk on a thin fence. All forms of equilibrioception are essentially the detection of acceleration.

21. Students that paddle balls against a wall or jump over objects with various heights are demonstrating which quality of movement? (Rigorous) (Skill 5.1)

   A. Balance

   B. Time

   C. Force

   D. Inertia

(C.) Force is the capacity to do work or create physical change, energy, strength, or active power. It is a classical **force** that causes a free body with mass to accelerate. A net (or resultant) force that causes such acceleration may be the non-zero additive sum of many different forces acting on a body.

22. Having students move in a specific pattern while measuring how long they take to do so develops which quality of movement? (Average Rigor) (Skill 5.1)

   A. Balance

   B. Time

   C. Force

   D. Inertia

(B.) Time is a sequential arrangement of all events or the interval between two events in such a sequence. We can discuss the concept of time on several different levels: physical, psychological, philosophical, scientific, and biological. Time is the non-spatial continuum in which events occur, in apparently irreversible succession, from the past through the present to the future.

TEACHER CERTIFICATION STUDY GUIDE

23. There are two sequential phases to the development of spatial awareness. What is the order of these phases? (Rigorous) (Skill 5.1)

    A. Locating more than one object to each object; the location of objects in relation to one's own body in space.

    B. The location of objects in relation to ones' own body in space; locating more than one object in relation to one's own body.

    C. Locating more than one object independent of one's body; the location of objects in relation to one's own body.

    D. The location of objects in relation to one's own body in space; locating more than one object in relation to each object and independent of one's own body.

(D.) The order of the two sequential phases to develop spatial awareness are as follows: the location of objects in relation to one's own body in space, and locating more than one object in relation to each object and independent of one's own body.

24. Coordinated movements that project a person over an obstacle are known as: (Easy) (Skill 5.2)

    A. Jumping

    B. Vaulting

    C. Leaping

    D. Hopping

(B.) Vaulting is the art of acrobatics on horseback. Vaulting is an internationally recognized, competitive sport that is growing in popularity. At the most basic level vaulting enhances riding skills. At any skill-level, this ancient dance between horse and rider deepens the sense of balance, timing, and poise for the rider, as well as a sensitivity to and respect for the horse-rider relationship. Vaulting in competition can be done individually or on a team of 8 people with up to 3 people on the horse at once.

25. Using the same foot to take off from a surface and land is which locomotor skill? (Easy) (Skill 5.2)

    A. Jumping

    B. Vaulting

    C. Leaping

    D. Hopping

(D.) Hopping is a move with light, bounding skips or leaps. Basically, it is the ability to jump on one foot.

26. Which nonlocomotor skill entails movement around a joint where two body parts meet? (Easy) (Skill 5.2)

    A. Twisting

    B. Swaying

    C. Bending

    D. Stretching

(C.) Bending is a deviation from a straight-line position. It is also means to assume a curved, crooked, or angular form or direction, to incline the body, to make a concession, yield, to apply oneself closely, or to concentrate (e.g., *she bent to her task)*.

27. A sharp change of direction from one's original line of movement is which nonlocomotor skill? (Easy) (Skill 5.2)

    A. Twisting

    B. Dodging

    C. Swaying

    D. Swinging

(B.) Dodging is the ability to avoid something by moving or shifting quickly aside

TEACHER CERTIFICATION STUDY GUIDE

28. Which manipulative skill uses the hands to stop the momentum of an object? (Rigorous) (Skill 5.2)

    A. Trapping

    B. Catching

    C. Striking

    D. Rolling

(B.) The ability to use the hands to catch an object is a manipulative skill. Catching stops the momentum of an object. A successful catch harnesses the force of the oncoming object to stop the object's momentum.

29. Picking up coins, tying shoes, and petting animals develop this nonlocomotor skill. (Easy) (Skill 5.2)

    A. Bending

    B. Stretching

    C. Turning

    D. Twisting

(A.) Bending is the process of bringing (something) into a state of tension: *bend a bow,* causing something to assume a curved or angular shape: *bend a piece of iron into a horseshoe,* forcing something to assume a different direction or shape, according to one's own purpose: *"Few will have the greatness to bend history itself, but each of us can work to change a small portion of events"* (Robert F. Kennedy), misrepresenting or distorting something: *bend the truth,* and relaxing or making an exception to something: *bend a rule to allow more members into the club.*

TEACHER CERTIFICATION STUDY GUIDE

30. To enhance skill and strategy performance for striking or throwing objects, for catching or collecting objects, and for carrying and propelling objects, students must first learn techniques for: (Rigorous) (Skill 5.2)

    A. Offense

    B. Defense

    C. Controlling objects

    D. Continuous play of objects

(C.) For enhancing the catching, throwing, carrying, or propelling of objects, a student must learn how to control the objects. The control gives the player a sense of the object. Thus, offense, defense, and continuous play come naturally as they are part of the controlling process.

31. Which of the following is not a type of tournament? (Average Rigor) (Skill 5.2)

    A. Spiderweb

    B. Pyramid

    C. Spiral

    D. Round Robin

(C.) A spiral is not a type of tournament.

32. Which of the following is not a type of meet? (Average Rigor) (Skill 5.2)

    A. Extramural

    B. Intramural

    C. Interscholastic

    D. Ladder

(D.) A ladder is not a type of meet.

33. Equilibrium is maintained as long as: (Average Rigor) (Skill 5.5)

A. Body segments are moved independently.

B. The center of gravity is over the base of support

C. Force is applied to the base of support.

D. The center of gravity is lowered.

(B.) Equilibrium is a condition in which all acting influences are canceled by others, resulting in a stable, balanced, or unchanging system. It allows humans and animals to walk without falling. An object maintains equilibrium as long as its center of gravity is over its base of support.

34. Which of the following does not enhance equilibrium? (Average Rigor) (Skill 5.5)

A. Shifting the center of gravity away from the direction of movement.

B. Increasing the base of support.

C. Lowering the base of support.

D. Increasing the base of support and lowering the center of support.

(A.) Equilibrium is a state of balance. When a body or a system is in equilibrium there is no net tendency toward change. In mechanics, equilibrium has to do with the forces acting on a body. When no force acts to make a body move in a line, the body is in translational equilibrium. When no force acts to make the body turn, the body is in rotational equilibrium. A body in equilibrium while at rest is said to be in static equilibrium. However, a state of equilibrium does not mean that no forces act on the body. Rather, it means that the forces are balanced.

TEACHER CERTIFICATION STUDY GUIDE

35. **All of the following affect force except: (Easy) (Skill 5.5)**

    A. Magnitude

    B. Energy

    C. Motion

    D. Mass

(D.) Mass is a property of a physical object that quantifies the amount of matter and energy it contains. Unlike weight, the mass of something stays the same regardless of location. Every object has a unified body of matter with no specific shape.

36. **For a movement to occur, applied force must overcome inertia of an object and any other resisting forces. What concept of force does this describe? (Rigorous) (Skill 5.5)**

    A. Potential energy

    B. Magnitude

    C. Kinetic energy

    D. Absorption

(B.) Speaking of magnitude in a purely relative way states that nothing is large and nothing small. If everything in the universe were increased in bulk one thousand diameters, nothing would be any larger than it was before. However, if one thing remained unchanged, all of the others would be larger than they had been. To a person familiar with the relativity of magnitude and distance, the spaces and masses of the astronomer would be no more impressive than those of the microscopist. To the contrary, the visible universe may be a small part of an atom, with its component ions floating in the life-fluid (luminiferous ether) of some animal.

PHYSICAL EDUCATION K-12

37. The energy of an object to do work while recoiling is which type of potential energy? (Average Rigor) (Skill 5.5)

    A. Absorption

    B. Kinetic

    C. Elastic

    D. Torque

(C.) In materials science, the word elastomer refers to a material which is very elastic (like rubber). The word elastic is often used colloquially to refer to an elastomeric material such as rubber or cloth/rubber combinations. It is capable of withstanding stress without injury. Elastic is flexible, flexile, resilient, springy, and supple.

38. Gradually decelerating a moving mass by utilization of smaller forces over a long period of time is: (Average Rigor) (Skill 5.5)

    A. Stability

    B. Equilibrium

    C. Angular force

    D. Force absorption

(D.) Force absorption is a moving mass that has weight. By utilization of smaller forces over a long period of time, the force absorption has been produced. It decelerates gradually.

TEACHER CERTIFICATION STUDY GUIDE

39. **The tendency of a body/object to remain in its present state of motion unless some force acts to change it is which mechanical principle of motion? (Average Rigor) (Skill 5.5)**

    A. Acceleration

    B. Inertia

    C. Action/Reaction

    D. Linear motion

(B.) Inertia (ĭnûr'shə) is a term used in physics that describes the resistance of a body to any alteration in its state of motion. Inertia is a property common to all matter. This property was first observed by Galileo and was later restated by Newton. Newton's first law of motion is sometimes called the law of inertia. Newton's second law of motion states that the external force required to affect the motion of a body is proportional to that acceleration. The constant of proportionality is known as the mass, which is the numerical value of the inertia. The greater the inertia of a body, the less acceleration is needed for a given, applied force.

40. **The movement response of a system depends not only on the net external force, but also on the resistance to movement change. Which mechanical principle of motion does this definition describe? (Rigorous) (Skill 5.5)**

    A. Acceleration

    B. Inertia

    C. Action/Reaction

    D. Air Resistance

(A.) Acceleration is the change in the velocity of a body with respect to time. Since velocity is a vector quantity involving both magnitude and direction, acceleration is also a vector. In order to produce acceleration, a force must on a body. The magnitude of the force (F) must be directly proportional to both the mass of the body (m) and the desired acceleration (a), according to Newton's second law of motion ($F=ma$). The exact nature of the acceleration depends on the relative directions of the original velocity and force. A force acting in the same direction as the velocity changes only the speed of the body. An appropriate force, acting always at right angles to the velocity, changes the direction of the velocity but not the speed.

TEACHER CERTIFICATION STUDY GUIDE

41. Which of the following mechanical principles of motion states that every motion has a similar, contrasting response? (Easy) (Skill 5.5)

    A. Acceleration

    B. Inertia

    C. Action/Reaction

    D. Centripetal force

(**C.**) The principle of action/reaction is an assertion about the nature of motion from which we can determine the trajectory of an object subject to forces. The path of an object yields a stationary value for a quantity called the **action**. Thus, instead of thinking about an object accelerating in response to applied forces, one might think of them as picking out the path with a stationary action

42. Which of the following principles is not a factor to assess to correct errors in performance for process assessment? (Average Rigor) (Skill 5.5)

    A. Inertia

    B. Action/Reaction

    C. Force

    D. Acceleration

(**C.**) Force is not a factor to focus on in process assessment.

43. A subjective, observational approach to identify errors in the form, style, or mechanics of a skill is accomplished by: (Rigorous) (Skill 5.6)

    A. Product assessment

    B. Process assessment

    C. Standardized norm-referenced tests

    D. Criterion-referenced tests

(**B.**) Process assessment is one way to identify errors in the skills of an individual. It is one way to know the limitations and skills that every individual possesses.

PHYSICAL EDUCATION K-12

TEACHER CERTIFICATION STUDY GUIDE

44. What type of assessment objectively measures skill performance? (Rigorous) (Skill 5.6)

   A. Process assessment

   B. Product assessment

   C. Texas PE Test

   D. Iowa Brace Test

(B.) Product assessment measures the skills of an individual. This process is a methodical evaluation of the characteristics of your product or service in the eyes of potential users and customers. The two principle types of assessments are principle-based assessments and usability testing.

45. Process assessment does not identify which of the following errors in skill performance? (Average Rigor) (Skill 5.6)

   A. Style

   B. Form

   C. End result

   D. Mechanics

(C.) Instructors can use end results to determine errors. From the process assessment, we can clarify what the errors are or what was wrong in the specific study.

46. Determining poor performance of a skill using process assessment can best be accomplished by: (Average Rigor) (Skill 5.6)

   A. Observing how fast a skill is performed.

   B. Observing how many skills are performed.

   C. Observing how far or how high a skill is performed.

   D. Observing several attributes comprising the entire performance of a skill.

(D.) To determine the source of the error in the poor performance of an individual, we use observations of several attributes that compromise the entire performance of a skill. Instructors should observe limitations and mistakes and determine how to best address these problems to improve future performance.

TEACHER CERTIFICATION STUDY GUIDE

47. Which of the following methods measures fundamental skills using product assessment? (Rigorous) (Skill 5.6)

   A. Criterion-referenced tests

   B. Standardized norm-referenced tests

   C. Both A and B

   D. Neither A nor B

(C.) Criterion-referenced tests and standardized norm-referenced tests are both methods that can prove and measure skills in product assessment. They can help to prevent or lessen errors.

48. Product assessment measures all of the following except: (Rigorous) (Skill 5.6)

   A. How the student performs the mechanics of a skill.

   B. How many times the student performs a skill.

   C. How fast the student performs a skill.

   D. How far or high the student performs a skill.

(A.) Product assessment evaluates student performance and gives insight into how students can correct errors. Product assessment measures results. Thus, how the student performs the mechanics of a skill is not relevant to product assessment.

49. Instructors can evaluate skill level of achievement in archery by: (Average Rigor) (Skill 5.6)

   A. Giving students a written exam on terminology.

   B. Having students demonstrate the correct tension of arrow feathers.

   C. Totaling a student's score obtained on the target's face.

   D. Time how long a student takes to shoot all arrows.

(C.) Archery is the practice of using a bow to shoot arrows. Totaling a student's score is the only method, of the possible choices, that evaluates skill level. Choices A and B test knowledge and choice D is an arbitrary measure.

PHYSICAL EDUCATION K-12

TEACHER CERTIFICATION STUDY GUIDE

50. **Instructors can determine skill level achievement in golf by: (Average Rigor)(Skill 5.6)**

    A. The number of "birdies" that were made.

    B. The number of "bogies" that were made.

    C. The score obtained after several rounds.

    D. The total score achieved throughout the school year.

(C.) Instructors can determine skill level in golf by evaluating a golfer's score after several rounds. The number of bogies or birdies is not necessarily indicative of skill level because they are isolated events (i.e. the score on one hole). The player who consistently scores the lowest likely has the most impressive golf skills. Therefore, a player's score is the best way to determine his/her skill level. Finally, several rounds is a sufficient sample to determine skill level. An entire year's worth of scores is not necessary.

51. **Instructors can determine skill level achievement in swimming by: (Average Rigor)(Skill 5.6)**

    A. How long a student can float.

    B. How many strokes it takes to swim a specified distance.

    C. How long a student can stay under the water without moving.

    D. How many times a student can dive in five minutes.

(B.) Instructors can determine skill level in swimming by counting the strokes a swimmer takes when covering a certain distance. The arm movement, the strength, and the tactic to move quickly gives the swimmer an ability to swim faster. The ability to float, stay under water, and dive quickly are not relevant to swimming ability.

52. Instructors can assess skill level achievement in bowling by: (Easy)(Skill 5.6)

   A. Calculating a student's average.

   B. Calculating how many gutter-balls were thrown.

   C. Calculating how many strikes were thrown.

   D. Calculating how many spares were thrown.

(A.) Instructors can determine the skill level of a bowler by calculating the student's average game score. There is a possibility that some coincidences take place (e.g., bowling a strike). To check the consistency, we determine the average instead of looking at only the score from a single game.

TEACHER CERTIFICATION STUDY GUIDE

53. What is the proper order of sequential development for the acquisition of locomotor skills? (Rigorous) (Skill 5.7)

   A. Creep, crawl, walk, jump, run, slide, gallop, hop, leap, skip; step-hop.

   B. Crawl, walk, creep, slide, walk, run, hop, leap, gallop, skip; step-hop.

   C. Creep, crawl, walk, slide, run, hop, leap, skip, gallop, jump; step-hop.

   D. Crawl, creep, walk, run, jump, hop, gallop, slide, leap, skip; step-hop.

(D.)

LOCOMOTOR SKILL: A skill that utilizes the feet and moves you from one place to another.

PRINCIPLE OF OPPOSITION: When a step is taken with the left foot, the right hand is moved.

WALK: A form of locomotion in which body weight is transferred alternately from the ball (toe) of one foot to the heel of the other. At times one foot is on the ground and during a brief phase, both feet are on the ground. There is no time when both feet are off the ground.

RUN: A form of locomotion much like the walk except that the tempo and body lean may differ. At times one foot is on the ground and during a brief phase both feet are off the ground. There is no time when both feet are on the ground simultaneously.

LEAP: An exaggerated running step. There is a transfer of weight from one foot to the other and a phase when neither foot is in contact with the ground.

JUMP: A form of locomotion in which the body weight is projected from one or two feet and lands on two feet. Basic forms: for height, from height, distance, continuous, and rebounding.

HOP: A form of locomotion in which the body is projected from one foot to the same foot.

SKIP: A locomotor skill which combines a hop and a step (walk or run). The rhythm is uneven.

GALLOP: A form of locomotion which is a combination of an open step by the leading foot and a closed step by the trailing foot. The same foot leads throughout. The rhythm is uneven.

SLIDE: The same action as the gallop except that the direction of travel is sideways instead of forward. The rhythm is uneven.

54. Having students pretend they are playing basketball or trying to catch a bus develops which locomotor skill? (Easy) (Skill 5.7)

    A. Galloping

    B. Running

    C. Leaping

    D. Skipping

(B.) Playing basketball involves near constant running up and down the court. In addition, chasing is a good example to use with children to illustrate the concept of running.

55. Having students play Fox and Hound develops: (Easy) (Skill 5.7)

    A. Galloping

    B. Hopping

    C. Stepping-hopping

    D. Skipping

(A.) Fox and Hound is an activity that emphasizes rapid running. The form of the exercise most closely resembles a gallop, especially in rhythm and rapidity. It can develop or progress at an accelerated rate.

56. Having students take off and land with both feet together develops which locomotor skill? (Easy) (Skill 5.7)

    A. Hopping

    B. Jumping

    C. Leaping

    D. Skipping

(B.) Jumping is a skill that most humans and many animals share. It is the process of getting one's body off of the ground for a short time using one's own power, usually by propelling oneself upward via contraction and then forceful extension of the legs. One can jump up to reach something high, jump over a fence or ditch, or jump down. One can also jump while dancing and as a sport in track and field.

TEACHER CERTIFICATION STUDY GUIDE

57. What is the proper sequential order of development for the acquisition of nonlocomotor skills? (Average Rigor) (Skill 5.7)

A. Stretch, sit, bend, turn, swing, twist, shake, rock & sway, dodge; fall.

B. Bend, stretch, turn, twist, swing, sit, rock & sway, shake, dodge; fall.

C. Stretch, bend, sit, shake, turn, rock & sway, swing, twist, dodge; fall.

D. Bend, stretch, sit, turn, twist, swing, sway, rock & sway, dodge; fall.

(C.) Each skill in the progression builds on the previous skills.

58. Activities such as pretending to pick fruit off a tree or reaching for a star develop which non-locomotor skill? (Easy) (Skill 5.7)

A. Bending

B. Stretching

C. Turning

D. Twisting

(B.) Stretching is the activity of gradually applying tensile force to lengthen, strengthen, and lubricate muscles, often performed in anticipation of physical exertion and to increase the range of motion within a joint. Stretching is an especially important accompaniment to activities that emphasize controlled muscular strength and flexibility. These include ballet, acrobatics or martial arts. Stretching also may help prevent injury to tendons, ligaments, and muscles by improving muscular elasticity and reducing the stretch reflex in greater ranges of motion that might cause injury to tissue. In addition, stretching can reduce delayed onset muscle soreness (DOMS).

59. Having students collapse in their own space or lower themselves as though they are a raindrop or snowflake develops this nonlocomotor skill. (Easy) (Skill 5.7)

    A. Dodging

    B. Shaking

    C. Swinging

    D. Falling

(D.) Falling is a major cause of personal injury in athletics. Athletic participants must learn how to fall in such a way as to limit the possibility of injury.

60. Which is the proper sequential order of development for the acquisition of manipulative skills? (Rigorous) (Skill 5.7)

    A. Striking, throwing, bouncing, catching, trapping, kicking, ball rolling; volleying.

    B. Striking, throwing, kicking, ball rolling, volleying, bouncing, catching; trapping.

    C. Striking, throwing, catching, trapping, kicking, ball rolling, bouncing; volleying.

    D. Striking, throwing, kicking, ball rolling, bouncing; volleying.

(B.) Striking, throwing, kicking, ball rolling, volleying, bouncing, catching, and trapping is the proper sequential order of development for the acquisition of manipulative skills.

TEACHER CERTIFICATION STUDY GUIDE

61. Having students hit a large balloon with both hands develops this manipulative skill? (Average Rigor) (Skill 5.7)

    A. Bouncing

    B. Striking

    C. Volleying

    D. Trapping

(C.) Volleying is to discharge in or as if in a volley: *volley musket shots at the attackers;* s*ports,* and to strike (a tennis ball, for example) before it touches the ground. In a number of ball games, a volley is the ball that is received and delivered without touching the ground.

62. Progressively decreasing the size of a target that balls are projected at develops which manipulative skill. (Average Rigor) (Skill 5.7)

    A. Throwing

    B. Trapping

    C. Volleying

    D. Kicking

(A.) Children develop throwing skills (the ability to propel an object through the air with a rapid movement of the arm and wrist) by projecting balls at progressively smaller targets.

63. Hitting a stationary object while in a fixed position, then incorporating movement, develops this manipulative skill. (Average Rigor) (Skill 5.7)

    A. Bouncing

    B. Trapping

    C. Throwing

    D. Striking

(D.) Striking is the process of hitting something sharply, as with the hand, the fist, or a weapon.

TEACHER CERTIFICATION STUDY GUIDE

64. **The ability for a muscle(s) to repeatedly contract over a period of time is: (Average Rigor) (Skill 6.1)**

    A. Cardiovascular endurance

    B. Muscle endurance

    C. Muscle strength

    D. Muscle force

(B.) Muscle endurance gives the muscle the ability to contract over a period of time. Muscle strength is a prerequisite for the endurance of muscle. Cardiovascular endurance involves aerobic exercise.

65. **Students are performing trunk extensions. What component of fitness does this activity assess? (Average Rigor) (Skill 6.1)**

    A. Balance

    B. Flexibility

    C. Body Composition

    D. Coordination

(B.) The core component of trunk extensions is flexibility. Trunk extensions also indicate the body's capacity for full expansion and emphasizes areas such as the stomach, arms, and shoulder joints.

66. **Data from a cardio-respiratory assessment can identify and predict all of the following except: (Rigorous) (Skill 6.1)**

    A. Functional aerobic capacity

    B. Natural over-fatness

    C. Running ability

    D. Motivation

(B.) The data from cardio-respiratory assessment can identify and predict running ability, motivation, and functional aerobic capacity. However, it cannot predict natural over-fatness, as natural over-fatness is a part of the human body. It is not artificially developed like running ability and motivation.

67. Data from assessing identifies an individual's potential of developing musculoskeletal problems and an individual's potential of performing activities of daily living. (Rigorous) (Skill 6.1)

   A. Flexibility

   B. Muscle endurance

   C. Muscle strength

   D. Motor performance

(A.) Flexibility.

68. The ability to rapidly change the direction of the body is: (Average Rigor) (Skill 6.2)

   A. Coordination

   B. Reaction time

   C. Speed

   D. Agility

(D.) Agility is the ability of the body to change position quickly. Reaction time, coordination, and speed are not the right words to describe the ability to move quickly, as we always say that the goalkeeper is agile.

69. Students are performing the vertical jump. What component of fitness does this activity assess? (Rigorous) (Skill 6.2)

   A. Muscle strength

   B. Balance

   C. Power

   D. Muscle endurance

(C.) Vertical jumping assesses the power of the entire body. It shows the potential of the legs to hold the upper body and the strength in the joints of the legs. Balance and muscle strength are secondary requirements. Power automatically ensures these secondary requirements.

70. **Which of the following applies the concept of progression? (Rigorous) (Skill 6.3)**

    A. Beginning a stretching program every day.

    B. Beginning a stretching program with 3 sets of reps.

    C. Beginning a stretching program with ballistic stretching.

    D. Beginning a stretching program holding stretches for 15 seconds and work up to holding stretches for 60 seconds.

(D.) Progression is the process of starting an exercise program slowly and cautiously before proceeding to more rigorous training. Answer D is the only answer that exemplifies progression.

71. **Which of following overload principles does not apply to improving body composition? (Average Rigor) (Skill 6.3)**

    A. Aerobic exercise three times per week.

    B. Aerobic exercise at a low intensity.

    C. Aerobic exercise for about an hour.

    D. Aerobic exercise in intervals of high intensity.

(A.) To improve body composition, a person should engage in aerobic exercise daily, not three times per week. However, an individual can do aerobics for at least half an hour daily, he/she can exercise at a low intensity, or he/she can train with intervals of high intensity.

72. Which of the following principles of progression applies to improving muscle endurance? (Average Rigor) (Skill 6.3)

    A. Lifting weights every day.

    B. Lifting weights at 20% to 30% of assessed muscle strength.

    C. Lifting weights with low resistance and low reps.

    D. Lifting weights starting at 60% of assessed muscle strength.

(B.) To improve muscle endurance, a person should lift weights at 20 to 30% of the assessed muscle strength. Lifting weights daily is counterproductive because it does not allow for adequate rest. In addition, lifting at 60% of the assessed muscle strength can damage the muscle.

73. The most important nutrient the body requires, without which life can only be sustained for a few days, is: (Easy) (Skill 6.4)

    A. Vitamins

    B. Minerals

    C. Water

    D. Carbohydrates

(C.) Although the body requires vitamins, minerals, and carbohydrates to achieve proper growth and shape, water is essential. Without it, the body gets dehydrated and death is a possibility. Water should be pure, as seawater can cause kidney failure and death.

74. With regard to protein content, foods from animal sources are usually: (Average Rigor) (Skill 6.4)

    A. Complete

    B. Essential

    C. Nonessential

    D. Incidental

(A.) Animal protein is complete, meaning it provides all of the amino acids that the human body requires. Although animal meat is not essential to a person's diet, it is an excellent source of protein.

TEACHER CERTIFICATION STUDY GUIDE

75. **Fats with room for two or more hydrogen atoms per molecule-fatty acid chain are: (Rigorous) (Skill 6.4)**

    A. Monounsaturated

    B. Polyunsaturated

    C. Hydrosaturated

    D. Saturated

(B.) Polyunsaturated fatty acids contain multiple carbon-carbon double bonds. Thus, there is room for two or more hydrogens. Polyunsaturated fats are more healthy than saturated fats.

76. **An adequate diet to meet nutritional needs consists of: (Rigorous) (Skill 6.4)**

    A. No more than 30% caloric intake from fats, no more than 50% caloric intake from proteins, and at least 20% caloric intake from carbohydrates.

    B. No more than 30% caloric intake from fats, no more than 40% caloric intake from proteins, and at least 30% caloric intake from carbohydrates.

    C. No more than 30% caloric intake from fats, no more than 15% caloric intake from proteins, and at least 55% caloric intake from carbohydrates.

    D. No more than 30% caloric intake from fats, no more than 30% caloric intake from proteins, and at least 40% caloric intake from carbohydrates.

(C.) General guidelines for nutritionally sound diets are 30% caloric intake from fats, no more than 15% caloric intake from proteins, and at least 55% caloric intake from carbohydrates.

77. **Maintaining body weight is best accomplished by:** (Average Rigor) (Skill 6.4)

    A. Dieting

    B. Aerobic exercise

    C. Lifting weights

    D. Equalizing caloric intake relative to output

(D.) The best way to maintain a body weight is by balancing caloric intake and output. Extensive dieting (caloric restriction) is not a good option as this would result in weakness. Exercise is part of the output process that helps balance caloric input and output.

78. **Most high-protein diets:** (Average Rigor) (Skill 6.4)

    A. Are high in cholesterol

    B. Are high in saturated fats

    C. Require vitamin and mineral supplements

    D. All of the above

(D.) High-protein diets are high in cholesterol, saturated fats, and they require vitamin and mineral supplements.

79. **Which one of the following statements about low-calorie diets is false?** (Rigorous) (Skill 6.4)

    A. Most people who "diet only" regain the weight they lose.

    B. They are the way most people try to lose weight.

    C. They make weight control easier.

    D. They lead to excess worry about weight, food, and eating.

(C.) People who participate in low-calorie diets do not control their weight easily. They must work more and utilize their bodies in many other ways (e.g., walking) to keep themselves fit.

TEACHER CERTIFICATION STUDY GUIDE

80. **Using the Karvonen Formula, compute the 60% - 80% THR for a 16-year old student with a RHR of 60. (Rigorous) (Skill 6.6)**

    A. 122-163 beats per minute

    B. 130-168 beats per minute

    C. 142-170 beats per minute

    D. 146-175 beats per minute

(D.)
220 – 16 (age) = 204, 204 – 60 (RHR) = 144, 144 x .60 (low end of heart range) = 86, 86 + 60 (RHR) = **146 (bottom of THR)**

220 – 16 (age) = 204, 204 – 60 (RHR) = 144, 144 x 0.80 (high end of heart range) = 115, 115 + (RHR) = **175 (top of THR) 146-175 beats per minute is the 60%-80% THR.**

81. **Using Cooper's Formula, compute the THR for a 15-year old student. (Rigorous) (Skill 6.6)**

    A. 120-153 beats per minute

    B. 123-164 beats per minute

    C. 135-169 beats per minute

    D. 147-176 beats per minute

(B.) 123-164 beats per minute.

82. Aerobic dance develops or improves each of the following skills or health components except… (Rigorous) (Skill 6.6)

    A. Cardio-respiratory function

    B. Body composition

    C. Coordination

    D. Flexibility

(D.) Aerobic dance does not develop flexibility, as flexibility results from stretching and not aerobic exercise. Ballet dancing, however, does develop flexibility. Aerobic dance develops cardio-respiratory function due to the unusual body movements performed. It also improves body composition and coordination due to the movement of various body parts.

83. Rowing develops which health or skill related component of fitness? (Rigorous) (Skill 6.6)

    A. Muscle endurance

    B. Flexibility

    C. Balance

    D. Reaction time

(A.) Rowing helps develop muscle endurance because of the continuous arm movement against the force of the water. However, flexibility, balance, and reaction time are not important components of rowing. Rowing also develops the lower abdominal muscles while the individual is in the sitting position when rowing.

TEACHER CERTIFICATION STUDY GUIDE

84. **Calisthenics develops all of the following health and skill related components of fitness except: (Average Rigor) (Skill 6.6)**

    A. Muscle strength

    B. Body composition

    C. Power

    D. Agility

(C.) Calisthenics is a sport that actually helps to keep a body fit in by combining gymnastic and aerobic activities. Calisthenics develop muscle strength and agility and improves body composition. However, calisthenics do not develop power because they do not involve resistance training or explosiveness.

85. **Which health or skill related component of fitness is developed by rope jumping? (Average Rigor) (Skill 6.6)**

    A. Muscle Force

    B. Coordination

    C. Flexibility

    D. Muscle strength

(B.) Rope jumping is a good mental exercise and it improves coordination. Many athletes (e.g. boxers, tennis players) jump rope to improve coordination and quickness. Muscle strength is secondary to that.

86. **Swimming does not improve which health or skill related component of fitness? (Rigorous) (Skill 6.6)**

    A. Cardio-respiratory function

    B. Flexibility

    C. Muscle strength

    D. Foot Speed

(D.) Swimming involves every part of the body. It works on the cardio-respiratory system and it develops flexibility because of the intense body movement in the water. It also improves muscle strength as swimmers must move their bodies against the force of water. Increased foot speed is not an outcome of swimming.

PHYSICAL EDUCATION K-12

TEACHER CERTIFICATION STUDY GUIDE

87. A 17-year-old male student performed 20 sit-ups, ran a mile in 8 minutes, and has a body fat composition of 17%. Which is the best interpretation of his fitness level? (Rigorous) (Skill 6.6)

    A. Average muscular endurance, good cardiovascular endurance; appropriate body fat composition.

    B. Low muscular endurance, average cardiovascular endurance; high body fat composition.

    C. Low muscular endurance, average cardiovascular endurance; appropriate body fat composition.

    D. Low muscular endurance, low cardiovascular endurance; appropriate body fat composition.

(C.) A 17-year-old male who performs 20 sit-ups, runs a mile in 8 minutes and has 17% fat composition has low muscular endurance, average cardiovascular endurance, and appropriate fat composition. 20 sit-ups is a relatively low number. An 8-minute mile is an average time for a 17-year-old male. Finally, a body fat composition of 17% is appropriate.

88. Based on the information given in the previous question, what changes would you recommend to improve this person's level of fitness? (Average Rigor) (Skill 6.6)

    A. Muscle endurance training and cardiovascular endurance training.

    B. Muscle endurance training, cardiovascular endurance training, and reduction of caloric intake.

    C. Muscle strength training and cardio-vascular endurance training.

    D. No changes necessary.

(A.) The person requires both muscle endurance and cardiovascular training while keeping the other bodily intakes normal. An appropriate program would include moderate weightlifting and regular aerobic activity.

TEACHER CERTIFICATION STUDY GUIDE

89. **Which of the following conditions is not associated with a lack of physical activity? (Average Rigor) (Skill 6.6)**

    A. Atherosclerosis

    B. Longer life expectancy

    C. Osteoporosis

    D. Certain cancers

(B.) A lack of physical activity can contribute to atherosclerosis, osteoporosis, and certain cancers. Conversely, regular physical activity can contribute to longer life expectancy.

90. **Which of the following pieces of exercise equipment best applies the physiological principles? (Average Rigor) (Skill 6.6)**

    A. Rolling machine

    B. Electrical muscle stimulator

    C. Stationary Bicycle

    D. Motor-driven rowing machine

(C.) A stationary bicycle is the best option to support the body physically as it includes all of the operations related to an individual's body (e.g., movement of legs, position of arms, back exercise, stomach movement). Electrical muscle stimulators are very dangerous as they can cause muscles to loosen too much. Other machines may provide an unnecessarily extensive workout that is dangerous for muscles

TEACHER CERTIFICATION STUDY GUIDE

91. Working at a level that is above normal is which exercise training principle? (Rigorous) (Skill 6.7)

    A. Intensity

    B. Progression

    C. Specificity

    D. Overload

(D.) Overloading is exercising above normal capacities. Intensity and progression are supporting principles in the process of overload. Overloading can cause serious issues within the body, either immediately or after some time.

92. Students on a running program to improve cardio-respiratory fitness apply which exercise principle? (Rigorous) (Skill 6.7)

    A. Aerobic

    B. Progression

    C. Specificity

    D. Overload

(C.) Running to improve cardio-respiratory fitness is an example of specificity. Specificity is the selection of activities that isolate a specific body part or system. Aerobics is also a good option, but it deals with the entire body, including areas not specific to cardio-respiratory fitness.

93. Adding more reps to a weightlifting set applies which exercise principle? (Average Rigor) (Skill 6.7)

    A. Anaerobic

    B. Progression

    C. Overload

    D. Specificity

(B.) Adding more repetitions (reps) to sets when weightlifting is an example of progression. Adding reps can result in overload, but the guiding principle is progression.

PHYSICAL EDUCATION K-12

94. **Which of the following does not modify overload? (Rigorous) (Skill 6.7)**

　　A. Frequency

　　B. Perceived exertion

　　C. Time

　　D. Intensity

(B.) Time extension, frequency of movement, and intensity are all indicators of overload. However, exertion is not a good indicator of overload, because measuring exertion is subjective and difficult to monitor.

95. **Prior to activity, students perform a 5-10 minute warm-up. Which is not recommended as part of the warm-up? (Easy) (Skill 6.7)**

　　A. Using the muscles that will be utilized in the following activity.

　　B. Using a gradual aerobic warm-up.

　　C. Using a gradual anaerobic warm-up.

　　D. Stretching the major muscle groups to be used in the activity.

(C.) Warm-up is always necessary, but it should not be an anaerobic warm-up. The muscle exercises, the stretching, and even the aerobics are all helpful and athletes should complete these exercises within the normal breathing conditions. In fact, athletes should focus more closely on proper breathing. Athletes should engage in anaerobic stretching after activity, when muscles are loose and less prone to injury.

96. Which is not a benefit of warming up? (Rigorous) (Skill 6.7)

    A. Releasing hydrogen from myoglobin.

    B. Reducing the risk of musculoskeletal injuries.

    C. Raising the body's core temperature in preparation for activity.

    D. Stretching the major muscle groups to be used in the activity.

(A.) Warm-up can reduce the risk of musculoskeletal injuries, raise the body's temperature in preparation for activity, and stretch the major muscle groups. However, a warm-up does not release hydrogen from myoglobin. Myoglobin binds oxygen, not hydrogen.

97. Which is not a benefit of cooling down? (Rigorous) (Skill 6.7)

    A. Preventing dizziness.

    B. Redistributing circulation.

    C. Removing lactic acid.

    D. Removing myoglobin.

(D.) Cooling down helps the body to regain blood circulation and to remove lactic acid. It also prevents dizziness, which may occur after extensive exercises. The only thing that cooling down does not support is removing myoglobin. However, it can help myoglobin get a strong hold in the muscles.

98. Activities to specifically develop cardiovascular fitness must be: (Rigorous) (Skill 6.7)

    A. Performed without developing an oxygen debt

    B. Performed twice daily.

    C. Performed every day.

    D. Performed for a minimum of 10 minutes.

(A.) The development of cardiovascular fitness is not dependent on specific time limits or routine schedules. Participants should perform aerobic activities without developing an oxygen debt.

TEACHER CERTIFICATION STUDY GUIDE

99. **Overloading for muscle strength includes all of the following except: (Rigorous) (Skill 6.7)**

    A. Lifting heart rate to an intense level.

    B. Lifting weights every other day.

    C. Lifting with high resistance and low reps.

    D. Lifting 60% to 90% of assessed muscle strength.

(A.) Overloading muscle strength is possible by lifting the weights every other day or by lifting weights with high resistance and low repetition. Overloading does not cause or require an intense increase in heart rate. However, overloading has many other possibilities.

100. **Activities that enhance team socialization include all of the following except: (Easy) (Skill 6.10)**

    A. Basketball

    B. Soccer

    C. Golf

    D. Volleyball

(C.) Golf is a sport that has individual players hit a ball into a hole using various clubs. It is one of few ballgames that lacks a fixed playing area. It is defined in the *Rules of Golf* as "playing a ball with a club from the teeing ground into the hole by a stroke or successive strokes in accordance with the rules." Though golf involves social interaction, it generally lacks the team element inherent in basketball, soccer, and volleyball.

TEACHER CERTIFICATION STUDY GUIDE

101. **Physiological benefits of exercise include all of the following except: (Average Rigor) (Skill 6.10)**

　　A. Reducing mental tension

　　B. Improving muscle strength

　　C. Cardiac hypertrophy

　　D. Quicker recovery rate

(A.) Physical exercises can help improve muscle strength by making the body move and they can help provide quicker recovery between exercise sessions and from injuries. However, physical activity does not directly relieve mental tension. It might reduce tension temporarily, but chances are the tension will persist.

102. **Psychological benefits of exercise include all of the following except: (Rigorous) (Skill 6.10)**

　　A. Improved sleeping patterns

　　B. Improved energy regulation

　　C. Improved appearance

　　D. Improved quality of life

(B.) The psychological benefits of exercise include improved sleeping patterns, improved appearances, and an improved quality of life. Improved energy regulation is a physical benefit, not a psychological one.

TEACHER CERTIFICATION STUDY GUIDE

103. **Social skills and values developed by activity include all of the following except: (Rigorous) (Skill 7.2)**

    A. Winning at all costs

    B. Making judgments in groups

    C. Communicating and cooperating

    D. Respecting rules and property

(A.) Most athletes have a confident attitude after a big win and consequently expect many future wins. They have a feeling of confidence that makes them think they will have the power to dominate other teams. However, the ultimate goal of physical activity is social, personal, and physical development, not winning at all costs.

104. **All of the following are methods to evaluate the affective domain except: (Average Rigor) (Skill 8.2)**

    A. Adams Prosocial Inventory

    B. Crowell Personal Distance Scale

    C. Blanchard Behavior Rating Scale

    D. McCloy's Prosocial Behavior Scale

(D.) McCloy's Prosocial Behavior scale provided one of the earliest discussions on the influence of participation in sports and on the development of socially desirable character traits. Not surprisingly, large voids still exist in the knowledge about athletes' moral reasoning. One area that has thus far received little attention by social psychologists is the relationship between sport involvement, moral development, and aggression.

105. Educators can evaluate the cognitive domain by all of the following methods except: (Rigorous) (Skill 8.2)

A. Norm-Referenced Tests

B. Criterion Referenced Tests

C. Standardized Tests

D. Willis Sports Inventory Tests

(D.) The Willis Sports Inventory Test is the tally of all wins and losses of the popular basketball player, Willis.

106. Which is not a common negative stressor? (Rigorous) (Skill 8.2)

A. Loss of significant other

B. Personal illness or injury.

C. Moving to a new state.

D. Landing a new job.

(D.) Landing a new job is generally not a cause of worry or stress. In fact, it is a positive event. Personal illness, loss of a significant other, or moving to a strange state can cause negative stress.

107. Which of the following is not a skill assessment test to evaluate student performance? (Average Rigor) (Skill 8.3)

A. Harrocks Volley

B. Rodgers Strength Test

C. Iowa Brace Test

D. AAHPERD Youth Fitness Test

(A.) Harrocks Volley is a volleyball code for a popular player named James.

PHYSICAL EDUCATION K-12

TEACHER CERTIFICATION STUDY GUIDE

108. All of the following are Systematic Observational Evaluations except: (Rigorous) (Skill 8.4)

    A. Reflective Recording

    B. Event Recording

    C. Duration Recording

    D. Self Recording

(A.) Reflective recording is not a type of systematic observational evaluation. Event, duration, and self recordings are all methods used in systematic observational evaluations.

109. A physical education instructor anticipates and prevents potential injuries, watches for hidden injuries, and takes an injury evaluation of the entire class. Which of the following strategies to prevent injuries is the teacher demonstrating? (Average Rigor) (Skill 9.4)

    A. Maintaining hiring standards

    B. Proper use of equipment

    C. Proper procedures for emergencies

    D. Participant screening

(D.) In order for the instructor to know each student's physical status, she takes an injury evaluation. Such surveys are one way to know the physical status of an individual. It chronicles past injuries, tattoos, activities, and diseases the individual may have or had. It helps the instructor to know the limitations of each individual. Participant screening covers all forms of surveying and anticipation of injuries.

110. In regard to injury prevention, RICE stands for: (Easy) (Skill 9.4)

   A. Raise, Ice, Compression, Elevation

   B. Rest, Ice, Compression, Elevation

   C. Rest, Inside, Compression, Elevation

   D. Raise, Inside, Compact, Elevation

(B) After an injury, it is important as soon in healing to apply the RICE steps.

111. Which of the following is not a state standard for P.E. in Florida ? (Rigorous) (Skill 9.5)

   A. Students are required to dress out for P.E. in all grades and all public schools

   B. Students are to understand the benefits of physical fitness

   C. Students are to learn certain motor skills to the best of their abilities

   D. Students are to be exposed to a variety of physical activities

(A.) Not all school districts in Florida require dressing out for P.E. This is a district by district choice and not regulated by the State.

112. Although Mary is a paraplegic, she wants to participate in some capacity in the physical education class. What federal legislative act entitles her to do so? (Rigorous) (Skill 9.5)

   A. PE 94-142

   B. Title IX

   C. PL 94-142

   D. Title XI

(C.) It is the purpose of Act PL 94-142 to assure that all handicapped children have available to them, within the time periods specified in section 612(2), (B.), a free, appropriate public education that emphasizes special education and related services designed to meet their unique needs, to assure that the rights of handicapped children and their parents/guardians are protected, to assist states and localities to provide for the education of all handicapped children, and to assess and assure the effectiveness of efforts to educate handicapped children.

113. A legal wrong resulting in a direct or an indirect injury is: (Average Rigor) (Skill 9.6)

A. Negligence

B. A Tort

C. In loco parentis

D. Legal liability

(B.) A tort is damage, injury, or a wrongful act done willfully, negligently, or in circumstances involving strict liability, but not involving breach of contract, for which a civil suit can be brought.

114. All of the following actions help avoid lawsuits except: (Average Rigor) (Skill 9.6)

A. Ensuring equipment and facilities are safe

B. Getting exculpatory agreements

C. Knowing each students' health status

D. Grouping students with unequal competitive levels

(D.) Grouping students with unequal competitive levels is not an action that can help avoid lawsuits. Such a practice could lead to injury because of the inequality in skill, size, and strength.

115. Which of the following actions does not promote safety? (Rigorous) (Skill 9.7)

A. Allowing students to wear the current style of shoes

B. Presenting organized activities

C. Inspecting equipment and facilities

D. Instructing skill and activities properly

(A.) Even though the shoes are important in physical education, the emphasis on current shoe styles does not promote safety because they focus more on the look of the clothing.

116. Although they are still hitting the target, the score of some students practicing archery has decreased as the distance between them and the target has increased. Which of the following adjustments will improve their scores? (Rigorous)(Skill 10.1)

   A. Increasing the velocity of their arrows.

   B. Increasing the students' base of support.

   C. Increasing the weight of the arrows.

   D. Increasing the parabolic path of the arrows.

(D.) Increasing the parabolic path of the arrows will increase accuracy and precision at greater distances.

117. Some students practicing basketball are having difficulty with "free throws," even though the shots make it to and over the hoop. What adjustment will improve their "free throws?" (Average Rigor)(Skill 10.1)

   A. Increasing the height of release (i.e. jump shot).

   B. Increasing the vertical path of the ball.

   C. Increasing the velocity of the release.

   D. Increasing the base of support.

(B.) In this case, increasing the vertical path of the ball will help the students make more free throws. Increased vertical path provides greater margin for error, allowing the ball to more easily drop through the hoop. Increasing the velocity cannot work due to common sense. Finally, increasing the height of release and base of support are not viable options in this case because the students are having no problem getting the ball to the basket.

118. **An archery student's arrow bounced off the red part of the target face. What is the correct ruling? (Average Rigor) (Skill 10.1)**

    A. No score.

    B. Re-shoot arrow.

    C. 7 points awarded.

    D. Shot receives same score as highest arrow shot that did not bounce off the target.

(C.) When an arrow bounces off of the red area of a target, the archer receives 7 points, the value of the shot had the arrow stuck in the target.

119. **A student playing badminton believed that the shuttlecock was going to land out-of-bounds. The shuttlecock landed on the line. What is the correct ruling? (Easy) (Skill 10.1)**

    A. The shuttlecock is out-of-bounds.

    B. The shuttlecock is in-bounds.

    C. The point is replayed.

    D. That player is charged with a feint.

(B.) If a shuttlecock lands on the line, it is inbounds by the rules of badminton.

120. A mechanical pinsetter accidentally knocked down the only bowling pin left standing for a spare attempt, after clearing all the other pins knocked down by the first ball thrown. What is the correct ruling? (Rigorous) (Skill 10.1)

    A. Foul

    B. Spare

    C. Frame is replayed

    D. No count for that pin

(D.) When the mechanical pin setter touches a pin and knocks it down, there is no count for the pin because the pin fell because of mechanical fault and the player had nothing to do with it. The other pins count and there is no foul for the player.

121. The ball served in racquetball hits the front line and lands in front of the short line. What is the ruling? (Easy) (Skill 10.1)

    A. Fault

    B. Reserve

    C. Out-of-bounds

    D. Fair ball

(A.) If a served ball falls in front of the short line, it is a fault according to a rule that states that a ball must fall within the short line frame at the time of serving. It is not out-of-bounds as it is still within the limits of the pitch. However, it is also not a fair ball due to the service rule.

TEACHER CERTIFICATION STUDY GUIDE

122. Two opposing soccer players are trying to gain control of the ball when one player "knees" the other. What is the ruling? (Easy) (Skill 10.1)

    A. Direct free kick

    B. Indirect free kick

    C. Fair play

    D. Ejection from a game

(A.) Assuming that the soccer player didn't intentionally hit the other player's knee, the result would be a direct free kick. If the foul was intentional, the referee can eject the offender from the game. Minor offenses and offenses not involving contact result in indirect free kicks.

123. Two students are playing badminton. When receiving the shuttlecock, one student consistently stands too deep in the receiving court. What strategy should the server use to serve the shuttlecock? (Average Rigor) (Skill 10.2)

    A. Smash serve

    B. Clear serve

    C. Overhead serve

    D. Short serve

(D.) The short serve would give land short in the court so the opponent would not be able to reach the shuttlecock. Therefore, the short serve would win the point. A clear or overhead serve enables the opponent to hit the shuttlecock and continue the game. A smash serve runs a higher risk of falling out-of-bounds. Neither of these scenarios are goals of the server.

TEACHER CERTIFICATION STUDY GUIDE

124. A basketball team has an outstanding rebounder. In order to keep this player near the opponent's basket, which strategy should the coach implement? (Easy) (Skill 10.2)

   A. Pick-and-Roll

   B. Give-and-Go

   C. Zone defense

   D. Free-lancing

(C.) A zone defense, where each player guards an area of the court rather than an individual player, allows an outstanding rebounder to remain near the basket. The give-and-go, pick-and-roll, and free-lancing are offensive strategies that do not affect rebounding.

125. When a defensive tennis player needs more time to return to his position, what strategy should he apply? (Rigorous) (Skill 10.2)

   A. Drop shot

   B. Dink shot

   C. Lob shot

   D. Down-the-line shot

(C.) When a tennis player is off the court and needs time to return to his position, the player should play a lob shot. Down-the-line shots and drop shots are offensive shots and are too risky in this situation. The dink shot would allow the opponent to take control of the point.

126. An overhead badminton stroke used to hit a fore-hand-like overhead stroke that is on the backhand side of the body is called: (Rigorous) (Skill 10.2)

  A. Around-the-head-shot

  B. Down-the-line shot

  C. Lifting the shuttle

  D. Under hand shuttle

(A.) A shot played from the backhand side and over the head is known as an around-the-head shot. It is played when the shuttlecock is high and cannot be reached any other way.

127. A maneuver when an offensive player passes to a teammate and then immediately cuts in toward the basket for a return pass is: (Average Rigor) (Skill 10.2)

  A. Charging

  B. Pick

  C. Give-and-go

  D. Switching

(C.) In the game of basketball, a give-and-go is an offensive play where a player passes to a teammate and immediately cuts toward the basket for a return pass. Charging is an offensive foul, a pick is a maneuver to free up a teammate for a pass or shot, and switching is a defensive maneuver.

128. A bowling pin that remains standing after an apparently perfect hit is called a: (Rigorous) (Skill 10.2)

  A. Tap

  B. Turkey

  C. Blow

  D. Leave

(A.) A bowling pin that remains standing, even after a perfect shot, is known as a tap. Other options, like turkeys and blows, are not relevant to the standing pin.

129. A soccer pass from the outside of the field near the end line to a position in front of the goal is called: (Average Rigor) (Skill 10.2)

   A. Chip

   B. Settle

   C. Through

   D. Cross

(D.) Any long pass from the sides of the field toward the middle is a cross, since the hitter hits it across the field. A chip is a high touch pass or shot. A through pass travels the length of the field through many players. Finally, settling is the act of controlling the ball after receiving a pass.

130. A volleyball that is simultaneously contacted above the net by opponents and momentarily held upon contact is called a/an: (Easy) (Skill 10.2)

   A. Double fault

   B. Play over

   C. Overlap

   D. Held ball

(D.) In volleyball, if two players simultaneously contact the ball above the net, the ball is a held ball.

131. Volleyball player LB on team A digs a spiked ball. The ball deflects off of LB's shoulder. What is the ruling? (Average Rigor) (Skill 10.2)

   A. Fault

   B. Legal hit

   C. Double foul

   D. Play over

(B.) Since the spiked ball does not touch the ground and instead deflects off LB's shoulder, it is a legal hit. In order for a point to end, the ball must touch the ground. In this instance, it does not.

132. In 1956, the AAHPER Fitness Conferences established: (Rigorous) (Skill 11.1)

A. The President's Council on Youth Fitness

B. The President's Citizens' Advisory Committee

C. The President's Council on Physical Fitness

D. A and B

(D., A., and B.) The **President's Council on Youth Fitness** was founded on July 16, 1956 to encourage American children to be healthy and active after a study indicated that American youths were less physically fit than European children. President Eisenhower created the President's Council on Youth Fitness with cabinet-level status. The Executive Order specified "one" objective. The first Council identified itself as a "catalytic agent" concentrating on creating public awareness. A President's Citizens-Advisory Committee on Fitness of American Youth was confirmed to give advice to the Council.

133. Which professional organization protects amateur sports from corruption? (Easy) (Skill 11.1)

A. AIWA

B. AAHPERD

C. NCAA

D. AAU

(D.) The Amateur Athletic Union (AAU) is one of the largest non-profit, volunteer sports organizations in the United States. A multi-sport organization, the AAU dedicates itself exclusively to the promotion and development of amateur sports and physical fitness programs.

TEACHER CERTIFICATION STUDY GUIDE

134. Which professional organization works with legislatures? (Average Rigor) (Skill 11.1)

    A. AIWA

    B. AAHPERD

    C. ACSM

    D. AAU

(B.) AAHPERD, or American Alliance for Health, Physical Education, Recreation and Dance, is an alliance of 6 national associations. AAHPERD is the largest organization of professionals supporting and assisting those involved in physical education, leisure, fitness, dance, health promotion, and education, as well as all other specialties related to achieving a healthy lifestyle. AAHPERD is an alliance designed to provide members with a comprehensive and coordinated array of resources, support, and programs to help practitioners improve their skills and in turn, further the health and well-being of the American public.

135. Research in physical education is published in all of the following periodicals except the: (Average Rigor) (Skill 11.2)

    A. School PE Update

    B. Research Quarterly

    C. Journal of Physical Education

    D. YMCA Magazine

(A.) Each school has a PE Update that publishes their own periodicals about physical activities. It aims at helping the students to catch-up on what is happening around them. The school produces this update to encourage their students to become more interested in all of the physical activities that they offer.

XAMonline, INC. 21 Orient Ave. Melrose, MA 02176

Toll Free number 800-509-4128

TO ORDER Fax 781-662-9268 OR www.XAMonline.com

FLORIDA TEACHER CERTIFICATION EXAMINATIONS   - FTCE - 2008

PO#   Store/School:

Bill to Address 1   Ship to address

City, State Zip

Credit card number _____-_____-_____-_____   expiration _____

EMAIL _____

PHONE   FAX

13# ISBN 2007	TITLE	Qty	Retail	Total
978-1-58197-900-8	Art Sample Test K-12			
978-1-58197-689-2	Biology 6-12			
978-1-58197-099-9	Chemistry 6-12			
978-1-58197-572-7	Earth/Space Science 6-12			
978-1-58197-921-3	Educational Media Specialist PK-12			
978-1-58197-347-1	Elementary Education K-6			
978-1-58197-292-4	English 6-12			
978-1-58197-274-0	Exceptional Student Ed. K-12			
978-1-58197-294-8	FELE Florida Ed. Leadership			
978-1-58197-919-0	French Sample Test 6-12			
978-1-58197-615-1	General Knowledge			
978-1-58197-586-4	Guidance and Counseling PK-12			
978-1-58197-089-0	Humanities K-12			
978-1-58197-640-3	Mathematics 6-12			
978-1-58197-597-0	Middle Grades English 5-9			
978-1-58197-662-5	Middle Grades General Science 5-9			
978-1-58197-286-3	Middle Grades Integrated Curriculum			
978-1-58197-284-9	Middle Grades Math 5-9			
978-1-58197-913-8	Middle Grades Social Science 5-9			
978-1-58197-616-8	Physical Education K-12			
978-1-58197-818-6	Physics 6-12			
978-1-58197-657-1	Prekindergarten/Primary PK-3			
978-1-58197-695-3	Professional Educator			
978-1-58197-659-5	Reading K-12			
978-1-58197-270-2	Social Science 6-12			
978-1-58197-583-3	Spanish K-12			
			SUBTOTAL	
	/handling $8.25 one title, $11.00 two titles, $15.00 three or more titles			
			TOTAL	